WHARF STREET REVISITED

GW00750731

A HISTORY OF THE
WHARF STREET AREA OF LEICESTER

BY
CYNTHIA BROWN

Published by the Living History Unit, Leicester City Council
© Leicester City Council
ISBN 0 9521090 2 6

ACKNOWLEDGEMENTS

The Living History Unit wishes to thank all of the following for their invaluable help in compiling this book:

Mr P. Adams; Mrs F. Ball; Mrs E. Bantan; Pastor Rob Briars, Carley Evangelical Baptist Church; Mr F. J. Brown; Mrs M. Bryan; Mr E. Carvell; Mrs P. Chapman; Mr R. Coleman, Art Pattern Co.; Mrs D. Cope; Mrs B. Doughty; Mrs J. Elson; Mrs D. Goss (nee Dakin); Sue Grewcock, British Steam Specialities; Mrs N. Halford; Miss E. Hill; Mrs E. Hodgson; Mrs I. Holyoak; Mrs I. Johnson; Mr Knight; Mr H. Limbert; Mr T. Madelin, Art Pattern Co.; Mr E. Martin; Mrs G. Moulding; Mr W. Pyne; Mrs D. Rayson (nee Pyne); Mrs K. Rowley; Miss Z. Rubenstein; Mrs M. Rudkin; Mrs I. Smith; Rev. P.J. Smith, Santa Maria, Ca.; St. Matthew's Tenants' Association; Mr E. Tait; Mr E. White; Mr L. Wilkinson; Mr C. Wright; and Mrs M. Zientek. Particular thanks are due to Jean Williams and St. Matthew's Tenants' Association for permission to quote from the *St. Matthew's Oral History Project*.

We are also grateful to the following for permission to reproduce illustrations: British Steam Specialities, Leicester; Mrs Chapman; *Leicester Mercury*; Steph Mastoris, Harborough Museum, Leicestershire Museums, Arts and Records Service; Mrs Pettitt; Mr Pyne; Mrs Rayson; Mrs Rudkin; Mr White; George Wilson, Environment & Development Dept., Leicester City Council; Mrs Zientek & Mr J. Zientek.

Finally, thanks are due to other Living History Unit staff and volunteers for their own assistance, in particular Vince Holyoak for additional research and the laborious work of transcribing oral histories from tape; Pete Illson and Pat Simpson for help with interviewing; Colin Hyde for taking photographs, and reading and commenting on the text; and Ian Gregson for additional items of research.

CONTENTS

Typical houses alongside one of the area's many pubs, the Palmerston Arms on the corner of Denmark Street and Taylor Street (M & J Zientek)

INTRODUCTION

Large numbers of people in Leicester must know the Wharf Street area well, if only by reputation - and it certainly had a reputation. *"Oh yes, Wharf Street"*, is a common response to any mention of the name: *"that was a very rough area, you know. The police went round in pairs... and we kept well away from it"*. But how well did the people who kept away from Wharf Street really know it? *"Nothing like that... rubbish!"* was the typical reaction from people who claimed closer acquaintance, coupled with the advice to *"ask anyone who lived there"* and an injunction to *"tell people what it was really like"*. I did ask them, and after listening to a wide cross section of people who lived, worked or otherwise spent any length of time there from the First World War onwards, I can only conclude that Wharf Street really was very different from the popular image which many people still have of it.

The district commonly referred to as Wharf Street covers that area just beyond the city centre which is encompassed by Belgrave Road, Charles Street, Humberstone Road, and the line of the Great Northern railway to the east. The roads forming the boundaries are not seen as a part of the area, which was linked from east to west by a network of interconnecting streets, and from north to south by Wharf Street itself, the axis on which it turned. This is not my definition, but a reflection of the "mental map" agreed by the people who lived there.

According to a League of Nations report in 1936, Leicester was the second most prosperous city in the world, but little of its wealth filtered through to Wharf Street. On the contrary, it will be clear from the oral histories and other sources quoted in this book that the lives of its inhabitants were shaped in every aspect by poverty. The cramped and defective housing characteristic of the area was all they could afford. Lack of money limited their diet, their access to health care, to leisure and entertainment, and to education beyond a certain level. It made them the focus of the many charitable and religious ventures described in these pages; and of the reforming zeal of public health officials, who swept away the "slums", and in the view of many, much that was worth preserving besides.

There were two main phases in the development of the area. The first, starting in the 1820s at the lower end of Wharf Street, was linked closely with the nearby canal, foundries and gas works, and the need to house their workforce. In the 1860s, the sale of the Wharf Street Cricket Ground led to further development, spreading out from Humberstone Road end of the street and including industrial as well as residential properties. This expansion reflected the massive growth of population in Leicester during the 19th century, which was due largely to an influx of people attracted by the prospect of work. Around 17,000 in 1801, within the space of a century it was well over 200,000.

This was one of the most densely populated districts of the town in the later 19th century. In 1881, almost 20,000 people - over a fifth of the total population of Leicester - were living in the two parishes of Christ Church and St. Matthew, which embraced the Wharf Street area. The figure had fallen to around 14,000 by 1911, in line with a general shift in population from inner areas of the city to suburban developments, but it crept upwards again as the First World War brought an end to new building. This put added pressure on housing which was already overcrowded and substandard, as the graphic descriptions of living conditions which appear in this book clearly demonstrate.

In the circumstances, the public house had attractions beyond that of drink itself. In Wharf Street alone there were so many pubs that drinking a pint in each and staying upright was a challenge which none could meet - and still more were to be found in the smaller streets throughout the area. It was this maze of narrow streets which constituted the Wharf Street area to which "outsiders" did not go, for Wharf Street itself was classed as one of the main shopping areas of the city. People came from far and wide to buy hardware at Holyland's, clothes and furniture at Marvin's, furs at Jacob's, ladies' hats at Impey's and prime cuts of meat from Hillyer's or Gregory's Top Hat butchers.

Innumerable smaller shops were also to be found along Wharf Street, on Russell Square, and in almost every side street throughout the district. Often consisting of no more than the front room of a house, the latter were an integral and essential part of the community, a source of gossip, help and advice as well as cheap goods and credit. Equally essential to many families was the pawnshop, the scene of an endless round of Monday "hocking" and weekend redemption of anything from clothes and bed linen to household furniture.

However, "tick" and the "pop shop" were only two of the many and varied strategies for survival which are recalled here, before the "safety net" of welfare benefits was extended to more than a tiny minority. *"I'm not making out that there's no poverty now"* said one woman, echoing the sentiments of many others, *"but people think they're poor if they can't afford a car or a video or a holiday. They just have no idea of what real poverty is"*. Real poverty in the 1920s and 30s meant no shoes, brown paper soaked in goose grease to keep out the cold, and the constant fear of the bailiff claiming their few possessions in lieu of unpaid rent. Some families were *"really, really atrociously poor"*.

Ill health was both a cause and a consequence of poverty, but before the days of the National Health Service access to medical care was largely determined by the ability to pay. In Wharf Street, the minority with regular work and a reasonable wage subscribed to a Friendly Society or to "the Clinic" in Chester Street, run by the Leicester Public Medical Service. Others relied on home remedies or cheap patent medicines. Only the most desperate resorted to the free medical services provided through the Poor Law. Claiming "on the parish" still carried such a stigma that for many years the services which replaced it after 1930 had the same taint. Both here and in the case of a death, help was freely given by neighbours only too aware of the precarious line which separated them all from the Workhouse and the disgrace of the "pauper's funeral".

Charity was always a more substantial source of aid than poor relief or other forms of statutory benefit, whether dispensed in cash, or more commonly - to rule out its diversion to the pub or other unworthy cause - in the form of clothes, food, medical care or the fresh air and fun which constituted the annual children's "treats". Some people refused charity because it was seen as placing them under an obligation to the giver - to show gratitude at the least, or to demonstrate that they were "deserving" - but many could not have survived without it. The Ragged School Mission in Bedford Street was the major source of charitable help in the Wharf Street area, but local churches and chapels played an important part too. Much of the social life of the area also revolved around these institutions, particularly for children. Many attended Sunday schools and all kinds of weekday activities, and looked forward with great excitement to the annual anniversaries and outings - just as they counted the days to the Saturday "twopenny rush" at the cinema, to learn the fate of poor Pearl White, tied to the railway line with the train drawing closer and closer.

Many of the people who have contributed to this book grew up in the Wharf Street area, and childhood memories of school as well as leisure feature largely in it. For a fortunate few, education might be an escape from poverty and a means of moving up the social scale as adults. Very often, however, scholarships had to be foregone because the family could not afford the uniforms, travel and the other expenses which attended a grammar school education. It was accepted that most children would leave school at the earliest possible opportunity in the hope of finding work and contributing to the family budget. Assuming they did find work, it was at this point that the family might take advantage of a higher level of income to move out of Wharf Street to another part of Leicester. The slum clearance schemes of the 1930s and 1950s removed the option to stay, but while they might be happy enough to go, it is clear that many former inhabitants also felt a sense of loss when transplanted to their "palaces" on modern housing estates. This was not simply a nostalgic hankering for an imagined past, in which the memory has conveniently edited out the bad experiences, but a very real sense of being part of a "community". The word trips lightly and sometimes without much meaning from the tongue, but it might be defined as a feeling of being part of a group which recognises that its members have mutual rights and obligations. This is discussed in more depth in the conclusion to the book - but it is clearly a feeling which many people found, and still find, lacking in the areas to which they were "rehoused".

Having argued that Wharf Street was a community in this sense, it is tempting to add the words "working class", to complete the description. However, things were slightly more complex than this. While the majority of its inhabitants were clearly numbered among the working classes, it also embraced a significant element of the middle class, including shopkeepers, publicans, teachers, clergy and other professionals. Many shopkeepers, it is true, barely scraped a living, and the line dividing the lower middle class from the working class was always a fine one. Nevertheless, to a very great extent they saw themselves, and were seen, as an integral part of the community that was Wharf Street, and of the framework of mutual rights and obligations within which it operated.

This being so, it is perhaps safer and more accurate to describe this book as the history of a neighbourhood. *"In the course of time"* wrote an American historian in 1925*, *"every section and quarter of the city takes on something of the character and qualities of its inhabitants... The effect of this is to convert what was at first a mere geographical expression into a neighbourhood, that is to say, a locality, with sentiments, traditions and a history of its own".*

It requires a great effort of the imagination to equate the Wharf Street of today with the vibrant and busy area of the past, but it is hoped that this book will serve as a record of its own sentiments, traditions and history.

Cynthia Brown
July 1995

Robert E. Park, quoted in Bourke J*., Working Class Cultures in Britain 1890-1960* (1994)

Crowning the May Queen at St Matthew's Junior School, Chester Street, around 1948 (M Zientek)

Rudkin's boatyard near Syston Street around the turn of the century (Leicester Mercury)

IN THE BEGINNING

Wharf Street was laid out to link Humberstone Gate to the Leicester Navigation canal, and was originally intended to cut across Belgrave Road to the public wharf on its far side - hence its name. In 1793, Leicester was the largest town in England without access to a navigable waterway, a much cheaper and faster means of transport than road, particularly when moving heavy goods such as coal. Until the Leicester Navigation was completed in the following year, this had to be brought overland from the West Leicestershire coalfield, or after 1779, by the Erewash canal from Derbyshire down to Loughborough, and then again by road into Leicester.

MAY THE LIQUID STREAM OF FORTUNE ENRICH YOU

Proposals in the 1780s to extend the canal from Loughborough to Leicester met with much opposition, both from local landowners and from Loughborough itself, which found its position as a terminus very profitable. In 1791, however, the project was authorised by Act of Parliament, and the work completed three years later at a cost of around £80,000.

Leicester Navigation with the former Wolsey Works on Abbey Park Road in the background (Leicester City Council)

The Leicester Navigation ran from Chain Bridge in Loughborough to West Bridge in Leicester. *"May the liquid stream of fortune enrich you"* was the motto under the company's seal, and it certainly brought great benefits to the town. Attempts to link the Leicestershire coalfield to the canal were not successful, but the reduced price of coal brought from Derbyshire benefited local industry as well as domestic users, encouraging the opening of Cort's iron foundry in 1799 near the Belgrave Road wharf, and gas works on a nearby site in 1821.

Cheaper dyestuffs became available to the local hosiery industry, along with greater access to export markets through the Humber, and after 1814, through a link to the Grand Junction into a still wider network of canals. However, the Leicester Navigation became less profitable with the coming of the railways: first the Leicester - Swannington line in the 1830s, which brought still cheaper coal from West Leicestershire and revived the local mining industry, and then the Midland Counties line, which opened in 1840.

Nevertheless, it continued to carry industrial traffic for many years, and was last used for the purpose by gas companies in the 1950s. In 1932 it became part of the Grand Union Canal itself, and in more recent years the growing popularity of canal boating has given it a new lease of life.

WHAT'S IN A NAME?

The origins of the name of Wharf Street may be fairly obvious, but what about those of other streets in the area?

Like Foundry Square itself, on the opposite side of Belgrave Road, Britannia Street took its name from Cort and Bell's Britannia iron foundry, and was probably laid out soon after this was built in 1814. Wheat Street, shown on a map of 1828, was then on the very edge of the eastern part of the town, and may owe its name to the wheat fields nearby. At this time, Russell Square was still linked to Belgrave Road by an old bridle road, which later became Junction Road. Willow Bridge Street recalls another feature of the local landscape - the Willow Brook, or as it was commonly known, the "Morsey"[1]. Hill Street was called Sandpit Lane in 1815, but was apparently renamed after Dr John Hill, who kept a private lunatic asylum in Belgrave Gate in the early 19th century.

Other streets laid out around Wharf Street in the earlier 19th century bear the names of prominent figures of the day. Both Russell Square and Russell Street were named after Lord John Russell, the Whig politician and parliamentary reformer who introduced the Great Reform Bill into Parliament in 1832. Bedford Street, which appears on mid-18th century maps as Barkby Lane, commemorates Russell's father, 6th Duke of Bedford, who died in 1839. No doubt the names also reflect the political sympathies of the developer.

A number of streets dating from the later 19th century also owe their names to politicians prominent at the time. They include Palmerston Street, named after John Henry Temple, 3rd Lord Palmerston, Liberal Prime Minister when it was laid out around 1861; and Gladstone Street, which took its name from William Ewart Gladstone, who was Chancellor of the Exchequer at the same time, and later served four terms as Prime Minister. Along with Freehold Street itself, the leading radical reformers and Free Trade campaigners John Bright and Richard Cobden feature in the streets

---

[1]*There are a number of theories about the Willow Brook's nickname of "Morsey". One is that it is a corruption of the name of former owners of the fields through which the brook flowed - Moses in one version, and Moor in another. An alternative explanation rests on an old advertisement showing cases of shoes being wheeled onto a steam ship on the Willow Brook near a shoe factory in North Evington, leading to mocking references to Liverpool and the River Mersey*

SHE DARED ME TO DO IT

Despite the reputation of Wharf Street as a "rough" area, there were few serious crimes of violence there in the 19th century. One exception was the murder in 1876 by John Thomas Green of Lee Street of his wife Emma.

The couple had nine children, but according to the Leicester Advertiser they "lived very unhappily together, and had frequent quarrels through the culprit having formed an illicit acquaintance with a woman of Loughborough... he had also been much addicted to drink". On 17 August 1876, "when at work at the shop of Mr Clarke, gunsmith, of Humberstone Gate, he obtained a few bullets of slugs and a small pistol, under the pretence it was for his boy Willie to shoot birds".

Four days later he shot his wife in the neck as she sat at the tea table, but "on being accosted by several neighbours saying that he surely had not shot his wife, he as calmly replied that he had... saying to one that she had caused it all herself; and to another that he should be a happy man now that he had done it. 'She dared me to do it', he told the police, 'and I have done it'...". Green was hanged at Leicester Prison on 20 December 1876. Following his execution, the first to take place in the town for over 30 years, "a black flag was hoisted at the front of the gaol in the vicinity of which a crowd of several thousand persons had assembled".

developed by the Leicester Freehold Land Society, a body formed in 1849 to increase the number of working class voters by enabling them to qualify as "forty-shilling freeholders".

Several streets have royal or noble connections, among them George Street, dating from around 1815 and named for King George III. Upper George Street, a later extension, commemorates his successor George IV, the former Prince Regent who married into the House of Brunswick - from which another nearby street takes its name. Clarence Street recalls William IV, Duke of Clarence, and Denmark Street provides a later royal link, being laid out in the 1860s around the time of the marriage of Edward Prince of Wales to Princess Alexandra of Denmark. Jubilee Road commemorates the Silver Jubilee of Queen Victoria in 1887.

Eldon Street is named after a former Lord Chancellor, the first Earl of Eldon; while Brougham Street, dating from the 1860s, owes its name to another Lord Chancellor - the Lord Brougham of brougham carriage fame. Curzon Street, laid out by 1837, marks a connection with Gopsall Hall, near Twycross, home of the Howe and Curzon family, who were great patrons of Leicestershire cricket and no doubt frequent visitors to the cricket ground in Wharf Street itself.

Milton, Byron and Dryden Streets, at the lower end of Wharf Street and dating from the 1840s, are early examples of "literary" street names. The Leicestershire villages of Syston, Wanlip and Birstall gave their names to three more streets, while events further afield are recalled by Clyde Street, named after Lt-Gen. Sir Colin Clyde, Commander-in-Chief in India at the time of the Mutiny in 1858. Closer to home, Erskine Street is named after the Rev. H.D. Erskine, vicar of St. Martin's church, now Leicester Cathedral.

The redevelopment of the Wharf Street area in the 1950s and 60s swept away many of the older streets, and new roads on the St. Matthew's estate bear Indian and Canadian place names: Madras and Kashmir, Ottowa and Kamloops, Calgary and Vancouver, Edmonton and Montreal. Dysart Way, however, recalls another past local notable, the Earl of Dysart, owner of large areas of land at Stocking Farm and elsewhere in Leicester.

Cockshaw's 1828 map of Leicester showing the first phase of development in the Wharf Street area. The Wharf Street Cricket Ground can be seen at the southern end of Wharf Street (Leicester City Council)

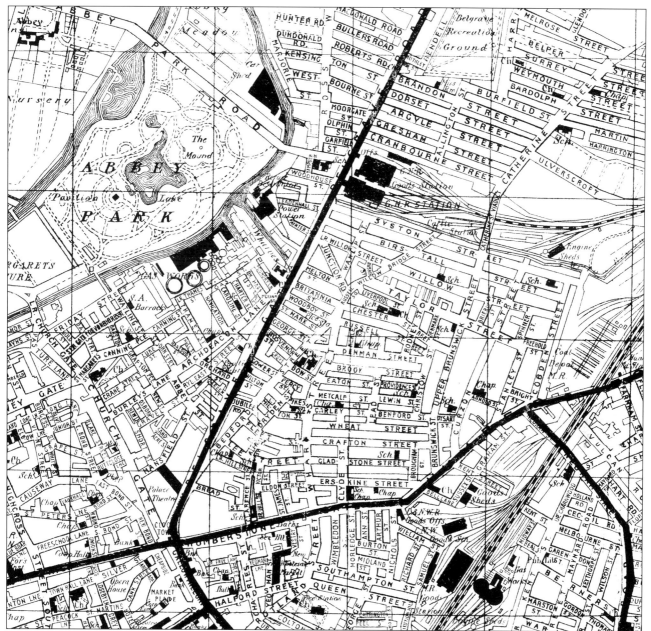

1907 map showing the development of the area following the sale of the Wharf Street Cricket Ground in 1860 (Leicester City Council)

15

WHARF STREET CRICKET GROUND

In the earlier 19th century, as new industry and housing consumed more and more open space , much of the outdoor social life of Leicester revolved around the Wharf Street Cricket Ground. This was situated between Wharf Street, Wheat Street and the rear of Spa Place on Humberstone Road.

Laid out in 1825, it was surrounded by a high brick wall fringed with poplar trees - but these *"greatly interfered with play"*, it was said, and they were lopped in 1845. The ten acre cricket pitch incorporated a bowling green, and was said to be the largest in the country outside Lords itself.

The ground was home to both the Leicester town club and the County club, and played host to many outstanding players of the day. Among them was Tom Gamble of Leicester, immortalised in verse after a combined Leicester and Sheffield team beat a Nottingham side by ten wickets in 1826:

For Tom kept hitting the ball in the crowd
Who in its applause grew boisterous and loud:
Then in praises of Gamble, grew equally mad -
Oh! thou'rt nought but a good one, little Gamble, my lad!

Ten years later, a North v South match at Wharf Street attracted large crowds from all over the country. Without the benefit yet of a railway link, hundreds of people were said to have walked from Nottingham, which had several players in the North team, *"and then had to toil all the way back to Loughborough to find sleeping accommodation"*. Playing for the South was Alfred Mynn, the 18 stone *"lion of Kent"*, who hit 21 and 125 not out despite an injured leg, and helped his team to a 218 run victory - but *"being unable to endure the agony longer, begged Lord Beauclerk to accompany him to one of the marquees... Lord Frederick instantly sent for a fly to convey him to the stage coach"*, and he was laid on its roof for an uncomfortable journey back to London.

In 1842 the Northern Counties played the MCC at Wharf Street, and *"great crowds flocked to see the game"*, many of them brought by special trains from Derby and Nottingham on the new Midland Counties railway. It was largely due to the efforts of William Barker, landlord of the Anchor Inn on the corner of Halford Street and Charles Street in Leicester, that this and other important matches were staged at Wharf Street - or "Barker's ground", as it was popularly known during the 20 years that he managed it from 1840. Though said to be notoriously mean with money, *"he lovingly cared for his ground, and... used to take the water cart round the ground on most summer evenings"*.

One of the more unusual games of cricket at Wharf Street consisted of a single wicket match in July 1846 between Lord Burghley, *"a cricket lover and a staunch supporter of this noble science"*, and Captain Cheslyn, *"the father of cricket in Leicestershire"*. According to the *Leicester Herald*:

"Both players meant winning, and notwithstanding the state of the ground, which was slippery from the heavy rain which was falling, both played remarkably well... the forty-eighth ball was

very hard and mounted. It was well-fielded by Robert Barker, and in his anxiety to get back the noble lord embraced the sod; and before he could recover himself Barker threw the ball from the long field, and scattered the stumps. Both players by this time were completely wet through, but were too 'plucky' to give in...".

The match was won by Lord Burghley on the second innings by one run, *"it being almost dark"*, and was followed by dinner and *"a variety of suitable toasts"*. On non-match days the public had free access to the ground, and to a wide range of special events at other times. These included pony races, athletics meetings, firework displays, balloon ascents and brass band concerts. *"Wednesday last"*, reported the *Leicester & Midland Counties Advertiser* on 27 June 1846: *"was quite a holiday in Leicester, on the occasion of Mr Green, the celebrated aeronaut making his 328th ascent by the Nassau balloon from the Cricket-ground... people crowded to the ground, while hundreds could be seen bending their course towards the Spinney-hills, from which a good view was obtained of the balloon... its final ascent being delayed a short time, owing to the pressure of the crowd. The scene presented was most animating; the brilliant assemblage on the cricket ground, the thousands of spectators on the neighbouring hills, the town with its Churches and gardens beautifully thrown out by the declining sun, presented an appearance... which it is quite impossible adequately to describe".*

Brass bands were very popular in the mid-19th century, and the cause of much rivalry between different towns and villages. One such contest at the Wharf Street ground in August 1859 attracted bands from Stamford, Thrapston, Northampton, Hinckley and Shepshed, and *"drew together at least 5000 or 6000 people ...".* The first prize of £12 was won by the Northampton Band.

The local Pensioners, military reservists *"who were more than once a useful addition to the police in riotous times"*, were regularly drilled on the Wharf Street ground, and an unusual event took place there after the general election of 1831, at the height of the campaign for the reform of Parliament. The return of Liberal candidates for both town and county in the general election of that year having caused *"great satisfaction"*, the newly elected Borough MPs, Messrs. Evans and Ellis *"gave a public dinner... at which upwards of 3000 guests were entertained. The sight was witnessed by a great concourse of spectators, and the proceedings were enlivened with music supplied by an orchestra of 250 instrumental and vocal performers".*

By 1860, however, William Barker's health was failing, and the Wharf Street Cricket Ground fell victim in turn to the demands of a rapidly growing town for industry and working class housing. The last cricket match was played there in September 1860 against an All England eleven, and on 7 November 1860 the ground and adjoining land along with two houses in Spa Place were sold by auction at the Bell Hotel in Humberstone Gate. They were bought for £5,600 by Samuel Stone, Town Clerk of Leicester from 1837 - 72, and the land was quickly built over. *"Vast number of houses have been erected in the last five years"*, reported the *Leicester Advertiser* on 7 October 1865, *"and their number is continually increasing. They are inhabited mostly by artisans, labourers and their employers; those of the former classes necessarily being much more numerous than the latter".*

THE POOREST OF THE POOR

Between 1801 and 1831, the population of Leicester more than doubled from 16,953 to 38,904, as large numbers of people moved into the town in search of work. By 1831 a number of closely built-up streets were clustered at the lower end of Wharf Street to cater for the demand for working class housing.

Initially at least, many of their inhabitants were probably labourers employed by the nearby canal, iron works or gas works. No doubt others were employed in the hosiery trade, Leicester's only other substantial industry, but one notorious at this time for low wages and high rates of bankruptcy.

The former Victoria Model Lodging House in Britannia Street, with detail of the panels (Leicester City Council)

The lodging houses and low rent housing in the Wharf Street area attracted some of the poorest of the poor. Joseph Dare, in the annual reports of the Leicester Domestic Mission, described their occupants as tramps, pedlars and migrant workers, but many of the latter would have been newcomers to the town, looking for work and unable to afford other accommodation until they found it. Similarly, in the 1920s and 30s, local lodging houses often accommodated young men tramping the country in search of work, attracted to Leicester by its relatively low level of unemployment.

The quality of the accommodation did vary, however, ranging from overcrowded buildings lacking basic amenities, to those provided by the Victoria Model Lodging House, built in Britannia Street in 1887 for its proprietor Mr Harry Wilkinson. The Victoria operated strict rules: no gambling, no alcohol, no smoking upstairs, no admission after 11 pm, and no female visitors. The occupants paid 4d (1.7p) for a bed, or 8d (3.4p) for a private cubicle, and a refundable deposit of 6d (2.5p) for the key to a cupboard. They bought their own food, but crockery and cooking utensils were provided, and according to an article in The Wyvern in 1895, *"the cooking ranges would not shame a Stoneygate mansion"*. Its owner also converted other properties in Britannia Street into hostels for destitute families and single women with children. According to the same article, *"Mr Wilkinson's 'Models' are indeed palaces"* by comparison with some of the lodging houses in the area.

The Victoria, which was sold in 1950 and converted into a footwear factory, has two carved brick panels on its frontage depicting the four nationalities of the British Isles: a Scotsman with umbrella and kilt next to an Irishman with a shillelagh; and John Bull standing alongside a Welshman holding a leek. It is now a hosiery factory.

Those fortunate enough to find regular work might eventually progress up the housing scale to more spacious, better built accommodation. Otherwise, they tended to exchange one mean and cramped dwelling for another marginally better or worse, according to their fluctuating fortunes. Tom Barclay, the son of Irish immigrants to Leicester, described a typical house of the later 19th century in his *Memoirs and Medleys: Autobiography of a Bottlewasher* (1934):

"After the monotony and dreariness of that Burley's Lane hut, I somehow find myself in a similar two-roomed hut in a similar court in a similar slum - Abbey Street... The scene changes once more, and we are again still in a two-roomed pigsty-crib in a court off Woodboy Street...

As with the previous dens, our door... was seldom open in summer and hardly ever in winter: it would never do to let the cold in... Two little rooms, one up and one down, and air, the air of a court too, having entrance and exit by one side of the house only... Poor as we were, we were not the poorest in the court; the very poorest were too proud to let the others know how poor they were".

JOSEPH MERRICK THE "ELEPHANT MAN"

Joseph Carey Merrick was born in Lee Street, between Wharf Street and Bedford Street, in August 1862. He suffered from a particularly severe form of an hereditary disease, causing a loosening and roughening of the skin, and tumours of the nervous and fibrous tissue - including the growth on the forehead which led to him being known as the "Elephant Man".

In his autobiography he wrote that *"the deformity which I am now exhibiting was caused by my mother being frightened by an Elephant; my mother was going along the street when a procession of Animals were passing by, there was a terrible crush of people to see them, and unfortunately she was pushed under the Elephant's feet, which frightened her very much; this occurring during a time of pregnancy was the cause of my deformity".*

This explanation was in keeping with the beliefs of the time, and the incident itself may well have occurred. Wombwell's Menagerie visited Leicester as usual in 1862 for the May Fair, and it was customary to parade the elephants through the streets to advertise it. However, though unrecognised at the time, his condition was later identified as neurofibromatosis, otherwise known as von Recklinghausen's disease after the German pathologist who first described it.

His mother died when he was ten, and his father remarried soon afterwards. *"Henceforth"*, he wrote, *"I never had one moment's comfort, she having children of her own, and I not being so handsome as they... she was the means of making my life a perfect misery".* After leaving Syston

Street Board School in 1874, he worked for a time at Freeman's cigar factory in Lower Hill Street, but lost his job when *"my right hand got too heavy for making cigars... I was sent about the town to see if I could procure work, but being lame and deformed no one would employ me... my father got me a pedlar's licence to hawk the town... but my deformity had grown to such an extent, so that I could not move about the town without having a crowd of people gather round me"*.

Unable to support himself, he spent some time in the Leicester Union Workhouse before deciding to *"get my living by being exhibited about the country"*. He contacted Sam Torr, who kept the Gladstone Vaults in Wharf Street, and *"went in for Novelties"*. Torr made the necessary arrangements, and after being shown in various Midland towns, Merrick was taken to London by the showman Tom Norman, who had a string of exhibition shops in the capital. It was while being exhibited at one of these, in the Mile End Road opposite the London Hospital, that Joseph Merrick first met the surgeon Frederick Treves, who was at that time Lecturer in Anatomy at the hospital's Medical College.

> *"I was anxious to examine him in detail"*, Treves later recalled, *"and to prepare an account of his abnormalities... I made little of the man himself. He was shy, confused, not a little frightened... I supposed that Merrick was imbecile... The conviction was no doubt encouraged by the hope that his intellect was the blank I imagined it to be. That he could appreciate his position was unthinkable... It was not until I came to know that Merrick was highly intelligent, that he possessed an acute sensibility and - worse than all - a romantic imagination, that I realised the overwhelming tragedy of his life"*.

Following a disastrous Continental tour, when Merrick was abandoned in Brussels by his manager and had to make his own way back to London, Treves arranged for him to be cared for at the London Hospital. He was supported by public subscriptions and the patronage of the rich and famous, among them the Prince and Princess of Wales, and the actress Madge Kendal. He died there in his sleep on 11 April 1890.

> *"As a specimen of humanity"*, wrote Frederick Treves, *"Merrick was ignoble and repulsive; but the spirit of Merrick, if it could be seen in the form of the living, would assume the figure of an upstanding and heroic man, smooth browed and clean of limb, and with eyes that flashed undaunted courage. His tortured journey had come to an end. All the way he, like another, had borne on his back a burden almost too grievous to bear..."*.

For a full account of Joseph Merrick's life, see Howell M. & Ford P., *The True History of the Elephant Man* (1980).

HOUSE AND HOME

The houses in the Wharf Street area were owned by a variety of private landlords, some with just one or two properties, others with larger holdings spread over several streets. The great majority were built before the introduction of local bye-laws laying down minimum standards for new housing, and while the Council had some powers to deal with insanitary dwellings, the condition in which they were maintained was still very much a matter for the individual landlord.

AT THE BOTTOM END...

Backs of houses in Wharf Street in the mid 1950s (Leicester Mercury)

By the 1930s, many of the oldest houses had serious structural defects, graphically described by the Medical Officer of Health (MOH) in his annual reports.

In Upper George Street, for instance, *"These houses are over 100 years old; two of them are of the one up and one down type... The external walls of the rear and gable are only four and a half inches (half-brick) in thickness, bulged and overhanging and very damp... There is only one water-closet and one tap in the yard for the joint use of three houses".*

Nearby in Bow Street, the houses *"are very congested, badly arranged and over-shadowed to the rear. They are very old, and there is evidence of serious dampness... no damp-courses are provided in the walls"*; and in Bedford Street, *"3 dwelling houses at a density of 83.5 houses to the acre. There is no secondary access to the yard behind these houses and the dust bins have to be carried through the houses to be emptied... There is no accommodation for the washing of clothes at any of the houses... all the rooms are dark and dismal, due to overshadowing by tall factory chimneys".* The worst example, however, was in a court off Belgrave Gate, where seven tiny dwellings housed 27 people. *"All these houses",* the MOH noted, *"are of the back-to-back type, situated in a little court entered from Belgrave Gate through a narrow passage. They are all in very bad condition".*

... AND THE TOP

Houses built later in the century around the top end of Wharf Street tended to be more varied in size than the older housing lower down the street.

In Carley Street, remembers someone who lived there between the wars, *"there were all different kinds of houses... mostly back-to-back terraced, but some of them were quite small, these little one bedroomed cottage type things which were built at the back of something else... all sorts of people lived in them... apart from the poor, there were also people that had come across to England as immigrants, you see... So you'd get the Italians, Russian, Jewish, a kind of mixture of everything... It was in the days when you could rent houses more easily"*.

Small houses were often built at the rear of larger properties. In 1922, for instance, the will of William Barrow, who owned several houses in Curzon Street and Russell Square, also refers to numbers 4-10 Chester Street *"and the five cottages in the yard at the back thereof"*.

A minority of houses boasted three bedrooms, but they were hardly spacious. In one such house, also in Chester Street, Mrs Elsie Hodgson recalls that *"up the stairs - it was a very long and narrow staircase - left hand side was the front bedroom, and you went through the back bedroom and into the real, little back bedroom... but over the other side of the road, they were what you'd call two-up, two-down"*. *"I was the youngest of nine brothers and sisters"*, recalled one contributor to an oral history of St. Matthew's estate*, *"and when I was very small I had to sleep with me two sisters, you see, there was three of us in a bed, then another, when four of us had to sleep in a bed, two had to sleep at the top where the pillows are and the other two had to sleep at the bottom where your feet were. That's how we managed"*.

A TYPICAL HOUSE

More typical were two bedroom houses such as the one described here in detail by Mr F. J. Brown.

We lived in Christow Street, which was in between Brunswick Street and Wharf Street, running parallel to both. As I remember, the house was owned by a Mr Hall, who I believe lived in the Evington area. The rent for the house was 7s 3d a week...

The whole side of the street was a continuous terrace, except for a back entrance to the New Leicester public house, whose front was in Brunswick Street... The houses, though joined as a continuous line, were owned by different people, some having two or three properties, others maybe more. We lived in a block of four houses... all four houses shared the one back yard, with the 'entry' to the rear in the centre, two houses on each side. The house itself had two rooms upstairs, and two main ones down, with a small kitchen attached, something like a lean-to shed. The two downstairs rooms were about 10 feet square, nine feet high. The living room had a red-bricked floor, as did the kitchen, while the front room had a wooden floor, with a foot space under.

St Matthew's Tenants' Association, *St. Matthew's Oral History Project* (1991)

A typical court of back-to-back houses off Belgrave Gate (Leicester City Council)

In the kitchen we had an old-fashioned sink under the window (which was very small). At the far end was the 'copper', a round, brick-built monster, and a small fire grate under it, so that you could boil your washing... Opposite the sink we had an old-fashioned 'stove' (cooker) with four burners, and an oven. This was made of iron... We had no taps inside, all water was got from a tap in the centre of the yard.

The tap was attached to the outer wall of the two toilets, one for each two houses. The toilets were in one 'shed', divided by a wall. They had straight-sided pans, and a wooden 'box' seat that took up the whole width of the toilet, and both had water tanks to flush them. The doors were three quarters the height of the opening.

The living room had an old iron fireplace about four feet square, the fire basket in the centre, and on the left side was an oven, heated by the fire. On the right side was a water bin with a lid, so we did have some hot water, though it only held enough to wash a few pots, then out to the tap in the yard with a big saucepan to refill it. Can you imagine what it was like in winter, when tap and toilets froze?

The lighting was by gas, an iron pipe from the ceiling looped into an 'L' shape, and had an incandescent mantle, which was very often broken when lighting up. You only had to touch it with the match, and it shattered. There was no shade over it.

The window was about five feet by three feet, a wooden 'sash' type, and next to that, in the corner, were two cupboards. That was it. The front room was more or less the same. Two cupboards. The bottom one had the gas meter, but the gas light was more modern, a straight hanging fixture, with a smaller mantle and a shade. The window was the same as the back one, and the front door opened to the street. The fireplace was small, with a small grate. The two upstairs rooms were the same as those downstairs in size. No cupboards, and only the front one had a very small fireplace.

The back yard was not divided, just a large open space for all four houses, and the toilets and tap were about 20-25 feet away from the houses in the centre of the yard up to the dividing wall of the houses in Brunswick Street. About 1935-6 we had the gas taken out, and electric lights put in, at a cost of about £16, and it was like this till the Council took over for demolition.

INSIDE, OUTSIDE

Better off families sometimes paid a local woman to clean their homes - anything from a few coppers for day to day cleaning to half a crown (12.5p) for spring cleaning the whole house. This was one way in which poorer families supplemented their income. Keeping these houses clean and doing the cooking when they lacked such basic amenities as an indoor water supply was hard work, which invariably fell on the women of the household.

The old-fashioned fire grate in the living room, remembers Ernie Martin, who lived in Eldon Street between the wars, was *"black-leaded once a week, and the hob on one side used to keep your food warm"*. Those people who could not afford a gas cooker did their cooking on the hob over the fire, while *"on the other side was a water butt, which got warm - but of course, it was always cracked, and we never had any hot water there... the fuel was under the stairs. The man had to come in with his bag and drop the fuel under the stairs... there was a door there. See, it was terrible, really. Anyway, we used to bank the fires up. We had plenty of 'slack', as we called it, little tiny bits of coal. Wet it, and it would keep in all day"*.

Though space was so limited, the front room of the house was only rarely used - for funerals, family gatherings at Christmas, or other special occasions. As Ernie recalls, *"the front room was THE room, it always had in the front window an aspidistra - they always did, everywhere you went, you must have an aspidistra on a stand in the front... You had a couch. We had a horsehair couch which I didn't like, because it used to prickle me. We had that and two chairs, and in the corner was a little cupboard where you put various things... in my Grandma's, I can always see, in her little cupboard, which was glass-fronted, were her false teeth...!"*.

In the poorest houses, the floors were often bare, but even in better off households, recalls Mrs Doris Goss (nee Dakin),whose family had a shop in Russell Square, *"there were no carpets, it was a peg rug, and we used to sell them for about three pounds... somebody had got to make them, see what I mean, by hand, with the bits of cloth. They used to have linoleum upstairs... and that went on for donkey's years - years and years. We never knew what a carpet was to cover the floor!"*.

At the front, most houses opened directly onto the street, although a few - in Gladstone Street for instance - had a garden with railings at the front. These went for scrap during the Second World War. Back yards, along with cold water taps, toilets, washhouses and a little patch of garden, were usually shared with at least three other houses.

Some houses had small patches of garden, where the choice of plants was much influenced by the closeness of the toilets as well as the lack of space - sweet-smelling plants which grew upwards rather than outwards were much favoured. *"Most of the plants grown in the small gardens were easy to establish in those conditions..."*, remembers one former resident, *"eg sunflowers, hollyhocks, sweet peas, delphiniums - in addition to 'creeping jenny' which was often put into window boxes and hanging baskets... and the chickweed for the budgies..."*.

"Entries" between the houses gave access to the yards from the street. *"In our yard in Lee Street was six terraced houses. It was all terraced - six in the yard. Three one side the entry, three the other..."*, remembers Mr D. Britten, who lived there in the 1920s. *"The yard was the length of the bungalows"*, recalls Mrs Beryl Doughty: *"We lived at one end... and the washhouses, where you used to do your washing, was up the top of the garden... Mother, you know, used to have an old table, and we used to keep our buckets of water on there, just for washing up, and we'd go to the tap for drinking"*.

"It was an awful way to live in one way...", said Elsie Hodgson: *"There were eight houses, and then there was the entry, and this side were four houses... we were lucky - we had a toilet for four families, but up the other end they'd got eight to one toilet and one tap, and we had a tap to ourselves... it was hilarious... winter mornings, either my Grandma or my Mam would be out, great*

big lump of newspaper flaming, up and down the pipe to unfreeze it so we could fill the kettle for more tea!". Other people had less orthodox ways of thawing it out. *"The tap used to freeze up in really bad weather"*, said one, *"and we used to pee on the top to unfreeze it - it's true!"*.

EVERY INCONVENIENCE

The great majority of houses in and around Wharf Street shared an outside toilet with one or more other properties. In 1923, according to the Medical Officer of Health, less than 20% of houses in the Wyggeston ward, which covered most of the area, had their own water closet, and almost 30% shared with at least two other houses.

The toilets also froze in cold weather, but this was only one of the inconveniences that had to be endured. *"I think we were a bit better off in Crafton Street than what they were further down Wharf Street"*, said Iris Smith, who lived there from 1929 until 1956:

> *"We had a tap in the house, and we had a toilet that we had to share with the people next door, which at the time was a way of life. But now I find it utterly revolting to think that you had to share toilets like that, and especially in the winter when it was dark, there was no light and you'd try to take a candle to the toilet, and I mean, nine times out of ten it would blow out because it was so draughty. I mean, the door didn't fit on the toilet very well. It was horrible... but at the time it was your way of life, and as I say, what you'd never had, you never miss...".*

There were other less common hazards. Harry Limbert recounts one story told to him by his father-in-law, P.C. Edwin Graham, who was patrolling with a colleague in 1920:

> *"One morning about 3 am they were walking past Melville Street when they heard a man shouting at the top of his voice... So switching on their lamps they entered a wide entry into a courtyard containing several cottages, and there stood a man in just his shirt and socks and he was wringing wet through.... It appeared he had got out of bed to go to the toilet, which was across the yard. He never bothered to put his trousers on, he walked across the yard in his shirt and socks, and when he was finished he pulled the chain and the water sprayed all over him. Someone had sawn the lead pipe that goes from the cistern to the pan, and pinched it...!".*

Finding the toilet occupied by someone else was no less awkward, but for at least one couple it provided a solution to the lack of space and privacy inside the houses themselves. As the St. Matthew's oral history recalls, *"The one toilet you couldn't get in very often as it was always occupied by next door, their eldest lad and his girlfriend at night used to lock the catch... What a place to do your courting!"*.

There were no bathrooms in the houses, of course, and without even an indoor tap, keeping clean was none too easy. *"Washing yourself in the morning was a nightmare"*, remembers Pat Chapman,

who lived in Wheat Street as a child: *"bowl on the table, topped up with hot water from the kettle, not fresh water for everyone. The family towel seemed to be used again and again. Motto: Get up early!"*.

As an alternative, said another, *"you washed in the kitchen in a little sink. Hot water you got from the cooker, and in the corner was a copper where you washed your clothes, and you would feed it with coal to get it warm, which I used to do when I was very young, and have a bath after the fire had gone out"*. Another familiar sight was the zinc bath, which *"used to hang in the outside shed at the end of the garden, and you used to have to light the copper... you boiled the copper up and filled the tin bath, and it was a case of you emptied a bit out and put some more in for the rest of the family... that was how you managed"*. Children attending Christow Street Board School between the wars could also have a bath at the school if they wished. One of the teachers, Mrs Rowe, was in charge of the "bath room", remembers Mr Brown, and *"how we used to look forward to the baths, as at home we only had cold water"*.

The only other alternative was the municipal baths, but these cost hard earned money. *"My mother gave me fourpence, I think it was, to go to the Vestry Street baths"*, Ernie Martin remembers, *"and you took a brown paper bag with your clean clothes in, and came out with your bag again with your dirty clothes in, once a week, which wasn't really enough, if you know what I mean, particularly if you worked in a dirty engineering factory"*.

Private landlords were largely free to charge what they wished in the way of rent, but this was dictated to a great extent by the ability of tenants to pay it. Once older children started work and began to contribute to the family income, some families were able to move to better accommodation elsewhere - but for others it was a constant struggle.

Average rents for a two-up, two-down property in the Wharf Street area in the 1930s were about 7s - 7s 6d (35 - 37.5p) a week, around a third of the average adult male wage. *"The rent was 7s 6d a week"*, recalls Pat Chapman of the family home in Wheat Street, and *"if you were in arrears ONE week you could be threatened with eviction"*. The "Bum Bailiffs", writes Dorothy Rayson (nee Pyne), were a familiar sight around Wharf Street, as *"rent was often in arrears. Whenever they appeared, the children of the area would shout a warning, 'The Bums are here!'. The bailiffs were powerful men. They had the authority to demand payment. If none was forthcoming, they could take out the few bits of furniture, put it onto the pavement, and change the locks. That is, if the family had not 'Done a moonlight' by removing themselves and their belongings to another district..."*.

Not that the bailiffs had it all their own way. They appeared one day when some neighbours were doing their washing, Dorothy continues: *"At the time, the two women were pushing clothes into the copper of boiling water with heavy copper-sticks. When the bailiff appeared, putting one foot in the door to prevent its closure, M.'s mother whipped round and thrust the hot copper-stick up the bailiff's trousers, singeing his bare leg. With a howl of anguish, the man retreated..."*. But he too had his revenge: *"Climbing onto the roof, he put a tin bucket over the roof to smoke out the inhabitants!"*.

CLEARING THE SLUMS

Apart from the flats opened in 1890 in Winifred Street, near the Infirmary, there was no Council housing in Leicester until after the First World War, when the Coleman, Saffron Lane and smaller estates were built. First and foremost, these were intended to ease overcrowding, which had become ever more serious as the war brought a temporary halt to house building.

On 15 May 1924, the *Leicester Mercury* gave some: *"SHOCKING EXAMPLES... PEOPLE HERDED INTO ROOMS SUFFERING UNTOLD MISERY... Overcrowding, due to the house famine, is one of the gravest social problems of the day. In one single room in Leicester a man and wife with their three children live and sleep. The Housing Department has turned their case down because it has been on the books for twelve months ONLY"*.

By the early 1930s, however, the situation had begun to improve, and with the aid of government subsidies for slum clearance, the Council was planning to replace the cramped, poorly ventilated and otherwise unhealthy housing in central areas of the city. The Wharf Street area fell into the Wyggeston ward, which in 1936 had the highest proportion of over-crowded properties in the city: an average of 5.4 people to each "structurally separate dwelling", compared with only 2.7 in the outer ward of Aylestone. However, clearing the area and rehousing the population was no simple matter. As the MOH Dr Killick Millard pointed out in his Annual Report in 1927, *"the people living in the small and worn-out houses, which are let at comparatively low rental, would often be unable or unwilling to pay the rent of a new house of the type which the Corporation have hitherto built..."*.

He estimated the lowest economic rent for such a house at around 11 shillings (55p) a week, including rates, but if this might be within reach of skilled workers in regular employment, unskilled labourers with dependents *"cannot afford to pay more than around seven shillings"*.

The Council originally intended to combine a programme of housing improvements with slum clearance. The worst houses were to be demolished, *"whilst the owners of many other houses will be called upon to repair and improve them...".* However, the planned improvements were abandoned following a new Housing Act in 1935, which also allowed the Council to use rents from existing tenants to subsidise rents of rehousing schemes. It was proposed to demolish 396 houses, 140 of them declared unfit for human habitation, and to replace them with 524 new homes.

Streets affected under the programme were Britannia, George, Bow, Bedford and Lee, along with parts of Wharf Street itself, where some houses were described as *"very old and generally in a worn-out condition. The internal and external walls are badly fractured and distorted and window and door frames are twisted out of shape, due to settlement of the foundations...".*

Most of the new houses to replace them were to be built at Braunstone and Northfields, on the outskirts of the city. However, slum clearance was not the only reason for the demolitions. It was a sign of the times - and of the rising incomes enjoyed by some sections of the population - that some of the land around Lee Street was also earmarked for a municipal car park.

Work on the new estates coincided with a fall in interest rates and building costs, and once started, it went ahead at a rapid rate. On 14 April 1938 the *Leicester Mercury* reported that: *"the 2000th family has this week been moved from Leicester clearance areas to the Corporation site at Braunstone under the re-housing scheme. Mr F.G. McHugh, Chief Sanitary Inspector, points out that the thousandth family was moved in February of last year, and to give some idea of the rate of removal, he explained that they have moved some 338 families during the first 15 weeks of this year, an average of 22.5 families per week".* However, the re-housing programme came to an abrupt end on the outbreak of war in 1939.

"One of the major social evils of our time which was in a fair way to eradication... is the slums...", wrote the MOH Dr E.J. MacDonald in his Annual Report for that year: *"One of the worst areas of the City, the Wharf Street area, was under active consideration at the outbreak of war, and but for this many very poor type houses would, by now, have been demolished".*

By 1939, around 2800 new houses had been built at Northfields, North Braunstone and on smaller Council estates to rehouse people from slum clearance areas. *"The Council had horse-drawn wagons that moved them, everything...";* but what did they think of their new surroundings once they arrived?

"It was marvellous", said one man who moved with his family to Braunstone in 1936 at the age of ten: *"There were only about 20 houses then, no roads, no lights in the streets, no shops. It was a long walk to the nearest shops - the park had railings then, so we had to walk round it, but the houses were like palaces, and the women kept them immaculate".* The *"wonderful thing about it",* said another early resident, *"was that we had a bathroom and toilet upstairs, which was very unusual in those days. But to have a bath with hot water and a gas boiler in the kitchen, it was marvellous!".*

However, other people found it difficult to adjust. In Bill Willbond's history of council housing in Leicester, *A Home of Our Own* (1991), one recalls that there were *"no roads, no buses - not anything. Even those who went to work in the morning had to walk down to the tram at Western Park, and I remember on the first night my brother Jack got lost. We were all worried stiff...".*

New municipal housing at North Braunstone, one of the estates which rehoused people from Wharf Street in the 1930s (Leicester City Council)

For children, there was *"nothing to do all of a sudden. Everything was new and shiny. You couldn't make a chock and play marbles in the street. There was one big advantage - you had a big garden. But the men took a big pride in them... and we weren't allowed on them".**

Wherever possible, the Council tried to rehouse friends and neighbours together. *"Out of the six of us... two families moved to Northfields... And the people in the yard, they lived next to us in Hanniford Road. They moved us together"*; but this policy, coupled with the Council's insistence on fumigating their furniture, gave rise to a popular view of both Northfields and North Braunstone as "problem" estates. *"To say you lived on Braunstone"*, said one woman, *"meant you were nothing... It was a case of give a dog a bad name"*.

Quite apart from the extra rent, the move often involved families in additional expense. There was the cost of transport to and from work, of furnishing and decorating a larger house, providing lino for the floor and paying for gas for lighting and cooking - with no hob over the fire now as an alternative. Tenants who could not pay the rent faced eviction. For some, the financial burden became too much, and they were forced to move back into cheaper private rented property. *"We weren't in Gipsy Lane for long"*, as one remembers, *"then we moved down into Lee Street, I think possibly because of financial reasons, really. I do remember that the rent in those days was 15 shillings (75p)a week. That was a lot of money...".*

*Quoted in Nash D. & Reeder D. ed., *Leicester in the Twentieth Century* (1993)

Houses and shops may be what first spring to mind when thinking of Wharf Street, but industrial premises - large and small - were also scattered throughout the area. This was a convenient arrangement, and typical of many working class areas in the 19th century. Employees were saved the effort and expense of travelling to work, while employers benefited from lower land prices on the fringe of the town, and a workforce almost literally on their doorstep.

SOCKS AND SHOES

Not surprisingly, many of the firms in the Wharf Street area were associated with Leicester's main industries - hosiery and footwear manufacture, and the engineering industry which grew up initially to supply both with machinery.

BSS advertisement 1946 (Leicester City Council)

The Burlington Works of Freeman Hardy and Willis, for example, were established in Erskine Street in the 1920s, and later became one of the company's warehouses. William Evans, another footwear manufacturer, opened his Belvoir Works in Bedford Street around the same time, moving there from Brunswick Street. In Clyde Street were the original premises of Coleman and Son tailors, now based in London Road. Its founder Simon Coleman emigrated from Poland to England at the turn of the century and learnt his craft as a foreman tailor with a Leicester company, setting up his own business in 1919.

In Wharf Street itself, W. Preston & Son Ltd. manufactured elastic webbing for boots and ladies' wear, *"for Home and Export to all parts of the world"*. India rubber thread was made by the Revere Rubber Co. in Birstall Street; needles at J. Ferriman and Co. in Erskine Street; and looms for elastic cord, webbing and braid by Thomas Taylor and Sons at their Gladstone Street Machine Works. J.C. Moore, based in Crafton Street from around 1890 until the 1930s, also made hosiery machinery.

Some smaller businesses occupied space between the streets at the back of houses. *"We had a great big entry"*, remembers Iris Smith, who lived in Eaton Street in the 1930s, *"because we had a factory in the yard"*. Horse-drawn transport was still in common use at that time, and her grandfather had a blacksmith's workshop at the top of Crafton Street. *"I used to love to go in there and blow the fire up with the bellows, you know... Bowles, the building people, were in Crafton Street, and I used to go with him up to Vipan and Headly's (in Gallowtree Gate) to buy his steel and whatever..."*

WILLIAM RAVEN AND CO.

It became less important to live close to work as public transport systems developed and a wider range of employment became available from the later 19th century. However, because of the time factor, many women with families still found it convenient to work near their homes. One of the largest and best known employers in the Wharf Street area was William Raven and Co.. The company was established in Crafton Street in the late 1860s, and later occupied large premises in Wheat Street.

Here, according to the *Homecoming to Leicester Souvenir* in 1910:

"The rooms are well-lighted, both naturally and artificially, and are both lofty and spacious... the immense plant comprises the latest automatic machinery for the production of all classes of goods, from a child's sock to the finest ladies' hose, plain or lace... As many as 900 operatives are employed by the firm, in addition to a large number of outside hands. The workpeople are classified under upwards of 18 heads, including rib hands, welters, rotary rib hands, menders, cutters, winders, seamers, leggers, footers and several others... The trade, which is both home and export, is strictly confined to wholesale houses. The exported goods are shipped chiefly to Australia, New Zealand, Canada and the Continent".

Wharf Street frontage of the former Raven's factory in Wheat Street (Leicester City Council)

A Liberal in politics, a Unitarian by religion, and *"a generous supporter of many charitable agencies in the town"*, William Raven himself was said to have:

"started life in humble circumstances, and by his industry and perseverance gradually built up a business not only of local importance, but ranking as one of the largest firms of hosiery manufacturers in the world... In spite of his advanced age, Mr Raven was actively engaged in the business almost to the last... (but) never sought to loom much in the public eye".

When he died in 1914 at the age of 82, the company employed around 1000 people, and continued to trade under the brand names of "Ravena" and "Craftana" until the 1960s.

GONE BUT NOT FORGOTTEN...

Although they have now ceased to trade, or have moved elsewhere in Leicester some of Leicester's most notable manufacturing companies originated in the Wharf Street area.

Among them was the Imperial Typewriter Company, first established in Wharf Street in 1908, before moving to East Park Road three years later. The company's machines were based on a design by a Spanish-American, Hidalgo Moya, who went into partnership with local businessmen. It specialised in machines with removable keyboards which could be interchanged to cater for different languages, and by 1914 around 95% of Imperial typewriters were exported. The company was later taken over by an American firm, and closed in 1975.

Charles Bennion, perhaps best remembered as the man who gave Bradgate Park to the City and County of Leicester in 1928, once had a sewing machine manufacture and repair business in Erskine Street. He was in partnership here in the 1880s with a Joseph Merry of Wharf Street, a silk and grindery dealer. With Marshall Pearson of Leeds, he later founded the firm of Pearson and Bennion,

Above: Art Pattern Co., Bedford Street, still trading after more than 100 years (Leicester City Council)
Below: The shop floor in 1987(Leicester Mercury)

which in 1899 was merged with others to become the British United Shoe Machinery Company on Belgrave Road. Bennion, who lived in Thurnby, was Managing Director of the BUSMC until his death in 1929.

The Bostik adhesive company, now in Ulverscroft Road, began as the Boston Blacking Co. Ltd., blacking, ink stain and rubber cement manufacturers, with premises at 88 Brunswick Street in the late 1920s. The Cascelloid company, now trading at Abbey Meadows as Cascelloid (BXL), started in August 1919 in a small four storey building in Britannia Street, in what was then *"an entirely new venture in this country"* the manufacture of celluloid toys, mirrors, bag handles, calendars and advertising novelties. However, in September 1927, when the factory was full of Christmas orders, it was badly damaged by a fire in which a young female employee died. According to the *Leicester Mail*, the fire brigade was:

"unable for some time to reach the attic floor, where the stock was kept, until it was too late to save the girl... At first it was believed that everyone was out until a roll-call was taken, when it was found that Miss Alice Salt, aged 17, 22 Chester street... was missing... The small grocery shop kept by Mr J. Prendergast on one side of the Cascelloid factory was literally flooded out, loaves and firelighters floating about in several feet of water...".

The company then moved to larger premises in Cobden Street before relocating at its present site in 1931 with investment from the British Xylonite Co. Ltd.

Many people will also remember William Colton's rope works in Crafton Street; the Besta soap works in Christow Street in the 1920s and 30s; and the Northamptonshire and Leicestershire Clubs Co-operative Brewery in Syston Street, which supplied local Working Men's Clubs with beer. The Wyvern Fountain Pen Co. also had a factory in Christow Street/Denman Street in the 1950s. The company moved to Woodboy Street from Calais Hill around the time of the First World War. Ernie White got a job there after leaving school in the 1930s, tapering the end of the pen barrels: *"A chappie showed me for a couple of hours, and later on that day the foreman came and said I wasn't turning out nearly enough, and he had another go at me on the Tuesday, and as I was on ten shillings a week - just think of it, what is now fifty pence - I politely told him what to do with his job"*.

…AND STILL HERE

Over 200 businesses were relocated from the Wharf Street area during its post-war redevelopment, but a handful of old-established companies still remain.

They include British Steam Specialities (BSS) in Lee Circle, manufacturers of equipment for steam, gas, water and other services. The company was founded at 5 Fleet Street in 1899, when steam was of course the predominant source of industrial power. In 1920 its premises were extended by the addition of six adjacent cottages, and again in 1933 by the purchase of an additional property for use as a garage. This became a nightclub in 1984, but replicas of the cottages, showing typical trades of the area, can be seen there. A new computer department was opened in Wharf Street in the 1880s, and BSS now has a total of 115 branches in the UK, with an annual turnover of almost £300 million.

The UK's leading manufacturer of press cutting tools, Art Pattern Ltd., is nearby in Bedford Street. Formerly the Art Pattern and Knife Co., the company was established by brothers J. and G. Cross in a small workshop in Birstall Street in 1887, and moved from the corner of Rutland Street to Bedford Street in 1935. Harry Limbert, who used to work there, remembers that:

"the Foreman of the knife shop, a youth named Mick, and myself would go to the new factory after ordinary working hours to build the forges and erect the shafting and motors... The week before Christmas I worked 30 hours overtime. My hourly rate was fourpence halfpenny... overtime was paid at time and a third, so I received 15 shillings overtime money, which nearly doubled my wages".

The Bedford Street premises were later extended, absorbing part of what used to be Fennel Street on one side, and the site of Duval's grocery shop on the other. Ron Coleman, one of the directors, and Theo Madelin, who has worked for the company for 53 years, recall that in a loft over the shop Mr Duval kept carrier pigeons which were used by the authorities to carry official messages.

William Hughes' shop at the corner of Russell Square and Woodboy Street in 1926 (Leicester Mercury)

WHARF STREET SHOPS

Some of the most vivid memories of Wharf Street are of its shops, which were so numerous that it is impossible to mention more than a fraction of them here. People came from all over the city to shop there. *"Every area in Leicester had its own Wharf Street"*, as Mrs Elsie Hodgson remembers: *"Spinney Hill had Charnwood Street, and so on. At the top end of Belgrave we had Catherine Street, but Wharf Street was THE shopping area"*.

EVERYTHING FROM A PIN TO AN ELEPHANT

In Wharf Street, it was said, you could buy *"everything from a pin to an elephant"*. Among the best known shops were Jacob's furriers, Impey's hat shop, Marvin's, and Frank Stevenson's furniture store, which also provided furniture for sets at the Theatre Royal in Horsefair Street.

"You could buy ANYTHING along there on a Saturday night up till ten o'clock, right down as far as Russell Square", said Ernie Martin:

> *"There were fruit shops, anything you like to mention you could buy along there, and the later it got, the cheaper it got... One of the most famous shops there, which was Cox's, and they used to supply wonderful breads and all sorts of pastries, cooked meats and everything... And then of course there was the great furriers, Jacob's, who had a wonderful shop at the corner of Erskine Street and Wharf Street. Now that shop was always full... And if you came a little bit away from there towards Humberstone Gate, there was Holyland's, the mangle people. They used to manufacture mangles galore, I can always see it there on the cast iron top, 'Holyland's - Leicester'...".*

Marvin's had two stores on opposite sides of Wharf Street - a general store near Bow Street and a furniture shop on the corner of Brook Street. *"They must have had at least six, I should think, plate glass windows..."*, remembers Elsie Hodgson, *"six all in a row, and they were always being broken, and I remember at Christmas they always had one devoted to toys. Oh! You'd stand outside with your nose on the window and your tongue hanging out, you know!"*. Marvin's *"sold almost everything!"*, wrote Dorothy Rayson: *"Clothes for the entire family, household linens and goods, even furniture. These items could be bought on Hire Purchase, which was much posher than the 'tick'...".*

The staff in this and other Wharf Street stores were said to be *"very obliging... you got personal attention. They got sacked if customers complained to the boss"* - but the work was poorly paid by

37

comparison with other occupations. In the 1930s, one woman recalled, *"I was going to work at Marvin's, but they only paid five shillings a week, and I could easily earn twice that in the hosiery".*

There were several drapers in the area, including Dakin's on the corner of Russell Square and Bedford Street, Elliott's at 188/190 Wharf Street, and William Hughes' haberdashery shop in Russell Square near Woodboy Street.

"As a teenager", Harry Limbert recalls, *"I had some smashing gear from that shop... two top coats at 30s (£1.50) each, and a trench coat - a raincoat - for 25s (£1.25). Shirts, socks and my work overalls all came from Hughes, and my 'Little Wonder' semi-stiff pointed collars were great at sixpence halfpenny each".* As a boy, someone else remembers a pair of trousers about 12 feet long hanging outside the shop with a sign saying *"If these trousers fit, you can have them free"*!

At Dakin's, Elsie Hodgson remembers, *"My Mam and Grandma used to pay four and eleven pence three farthings (25p) for a pair of corsets, whalebone things, you know. Really nice things... they had to be cheap in those days for people... I remember when my Mam paid threepence for a bag of doll rags, a great big bag of bits of satin and bits of silk, bits of shirt to dress my dolls in...".* Mrs Doris Goss (nee Dakin) recalled that:

> *"we used to sell a lot of caps to the men on a Sunday morning. They would go down the football Saturday afternoon and throw their caps in the air if they won! The women would refuse to go out with them without their caps... We'd also sell collars - separate - size 15, 15 and a half, you know. My Dad used to wear one of them, a hard front and a collar, had to be starched. We used to have a Chinese laundry, and then they had the imitation fronts, you know, the men used to, it wasn't a shirt, just what they called fronts".*

OPEN ALL HOURS

Many more smaller shops were to be found in the streets around Wharf Street itself. They played a central role in the life of the community, selling a great variety of goods, providing credit for poorer families, and acting as a point of contact.

Several of them, one former resident recalls, were run by *"old ladies who always wore a man's cap"*. Shopkeeping was one way in which women might support themselves after being widowed, but many were small family businesses, with children expected to help out by serving in the shop, running errands, and weighing and bagging up goods.

Until the 1950s, when their hours were more strictly regulated, many were open seven days a week. As one former shopkeeper pointed out, many people worked on Saturdays and were not paid their wages until the evening - so *"if we didn't open on Sunday, we would never have taken anything"*. It was *"absolutely lovely when we started to close on Sunday afternoons"*, said another: *"You never had any time to yourself until then. We used to make it when everybody went by to go to the Star picture house, you know, that was it! We said, we've closed!"*. In February 1930, Ernie White remembers:

Ernie White's father Bill, pictured outside the family shop in Brook Street in 1955 (Leicester Mercury)

For many years Bill White and his wife Elizabeth were Leicester's Pearly King and Queen. They are pictured here in 1932. Ernie White (right, against window) carried on the tradition (Mr E White)

"Dad had bought this little old shop down in Brook Street, off Wharf Street. Very run down, dilapidated place... and of course it was quite a lift up the ladder because Dad had had various jobs over the years, and this was something on his own... We used to open at about half past six in the morning till about eight o'clock at night, and it used to be up until nine o'clock or thereabouts on a Friday, seven o'clock on a Saturday and all day on a Sunday. You were in and out the shop all the time... and if you took in those very early days forty, fifty pounds a week, you were doing very well indeed...".

Ernie also remembers that "one man used to come in for a halfpenny fag every half hour. I asked him why he didn't come in and buy more for less money - five for twopence, Woodbines. He said no fear, he was trying to give up!". However, shopkeepers prided themselves on the service they offered to customers, many of whom were married women working in factories. Calvert's bakery in Russell Square "was a sight to behold in the morning, the women going to work, you know, they'd got the baking tins with their dinner... leave off at dinner, come home, flying home... and she used to charge them threepence a day for cooking their dinners in the big ovens". People also cooked their Sunday joints and Christmas dinners there.

"I used to soak peas", said one shopkeeper, "because we had all the factory girls. There was loads of working women in the shoe factories there, and they'd come and they'd have soaked peas. I used to scrape potatoes for them, beetroot... Now *when I think back, my husband, he'd do anything for those customers - well, I DID it!. But most of it was his idea"*. White's shop also sold soaked peas:

> *"We soaked 60 lbs, which makes 120 pints, EVERY day of the year including Christmas Day, and we never had any left. We used to cook bacon hocks... soak them overnight, then the next day we would boil them up in the old copper in the kitchen and sell them hot at threepence or fourpence each... People used to come and order these things! And then the next day the liquor that they'd been cooked in used to set solid, all this jelly, so we'd take the top scum off, and then we used vegetables... things like carrots and parsnips and things like that, and grate them up into the soup, boil it up again, and we'd sell that as hot soup on Friday at twopence a pint, and that really used to go like wildfire! I can see them coming in now with a jug of ale in one hand, and another jug, or even things that are unmentionable, for a couple of pints of soup!".*

Shops selling food were subject to periodic visits from Health Department inspectors, and these occasionally caused some resentment. One shop on Russell Square was *"so scruffy you couldn't believe it! And at one time the Health people hounded me, even come in and said 'How many times a day do you wash that?', you know. So, I mean, I got a little browned off because we was cleaning all the time. So I said 'Why don't you go around to Mr X's?'. 'Oh, he's co-operating now. He's getting all the cobwebs down', they said!...".* Was this the same shop which Dorothy Rayson remembers as *"the cheapest of the cheap, where none of the discerning customers would go. The wooden floor creaked, cobwebs festooned every nook and cranny, and dust lay on the cracked counter. It sold everything - greasy bacon, candles, firelighters, cheese, disinfectants...!".*

The supermarket was still a thing of the future in the 1930s, but there were a few "multiple" food stores in the Wharf Street area by then. They included branches of Kay's - "Kays Ways Pays" - Worthington's Cash Stores and the Leicester Co-operative Society, which had grocery or butcher's stores in Christow Street, Wharf Street and Chester Street. The dividend paid every six months on Co-op purchases was a welcome bonus for many families. *"Always reminds me..."*, Mrs Goss said, *"this woman went into the Co-op and asked for some bones for the dog. The butcher offered her them for nothing, but she said no, she wanted him to charge her as she wanted the 'divi' on them!".*

Ernie White went to work for Worthington's in Wharf Street in the 1930s as an errand boy. *"It might surprise a lot of people that there wasn't even a fridge in the shop"*, he said:

> *"One or two of the larger butchers had their cold rooms, but the majority of grocers didn't have a fridge, I think until about 1950... so you can see that when you got a very warm spell, your sausages used to go off a bit, so over the weekend, any that was left, we used to put them in a bath of water with some salt, and that would keep them nice and fresh over the weekend. You'd fetch them out, dry them off, and then they'd be coming in on the Monday morning for a pound of sausage. If I remember rightly, it was fourpence for the beef sausage and sixpence a pound for the pork sausage.*

"As the errand boy, of course, I had to do things like skimming the cheese and cleaning the currants, dry fruit, things like that. Fruit would come in large wooden boxes, and we would tip them in a sieve, sprinkle sugared water over the top and rub them - try and clean them up a bit. At the same time it swelled the fruit a bit, and I suppose it made them weigh a bit more. Anything that was going off, you'd get people coming in last thing Saturday night. We'd got things which were probably a bit too ropey to keep until Monday, and we would sell it off cheap...".

TOP HAT... AND TAIL ENDS

Many people will remember the "Top Hat" butcher's shop in Wharf Street, near Russell Square. Its proprietor, "Hoggy" Gregory, later became landlord of the Eclipse pub near the Clock Tower. The Top Hat was also one of the businesses advertised by the Billy Frizwell, the "Little Colonel", who was a familiar sight around Wharf Street before the Second World War.

"There was a little bloke called the Colonel...", recalls Mrs Goss: *"only four foot four or so. The Colonel - why? Because he was an old soldier. He used to have his medals and his top hat, and his board - 'Gregory, Top Hat Butcher, buy your meat today from him' - right, marching up and down, and he did his little stint. 'Can you see this? This is where you want to get your joint on a Sunday morning'. Well, he couldn't give his meat away - because he couldn't keep it, you see, there were no fridges. Never opened on a Monday, butchers didn't. And his place'd be packed, and he'd got a bit of sirloin - and this is the truth - about four inches thick, and he'd say 'What'd you pay me for this?'. No answer. 'Half a crown?' No answer! He'd say 'Missus, how many kids have you got?' She'd say 'There's about six of us'. He'd got no fridge, it'd go off, so he said 'Give it to her!'...".*

"We used to go down on Sunday Mornings to the Top Hat butcher's with five shillings and a note", someone else remembers: *"a piece of aitch bone, about five shillings, then he'd slap on a pound of sausages, a big slab of steak, a heap of bones and a lump of suet, all for five bob".*

Also in Wharf Street, on the corner of Bow Street, was Hillyer's. *"Hillyer's the pork butchers - now that was a nice shop... it was a family concern, you know, it was really good quality stuff, and when you went in they had these lovely kind of Windsor chairs for people to sit in - very civilised! We used to go in the shop just to sit on the chairs!"*. Hillyer's did a good trade in cooked meat from employees of nearby factories, like the Art Pattern and Knife Co. in Bedford Street - Ron Coleman and Theo Madelin well remember buying sausages and other food from there, fried in a copper full of fat!

At the weekend, recalls another, *"you'd see people running up to the butcher's with big pudding basins and a jug, and the jug was for faggots and gravy, and the pudding basin was for the pig's belly, you know, that sort of thing...".* Further up Wharf Street, towards Humberstone Road was Shield's pork butcher's, *"and they had pork, just plain pork, and you could buy your evening meal with roast pork, with that beautiful - on the edge - that beautiful rind. It really was very nice...".*

Farrow's, on the corner of Russell Square and Chester Street, was another popular local butcher. Near here was a slaughterhouse, and *"many a time I've seen them bringing the sheep down for slaughter, and they all used to herd in the yard, at the back of houses as well. I mean, thinking about it now, it was awful..."*.

Wharf Street was also well supplied with fishmongers - Mansfield's and Dexter's among them - some of which also sold poultry. The rows of turkeys hanging outside at Christmas were a familiar sight, and on Christmas Eve some would stay open until midnight to cater for last minute buyers looking for a bargain. There were several fish and chip shops as well. *"Cod, hake, plaice - plaice was very expensive"*, remembers Ernie Martin, but *"there was a fish shop just opposite the Callow Dairy... They used to sell round bits. 'Round bit and chips, please'. Fourpence, and it was a round bit of hake, beautifully fried, a bone in the middle"*. Even cheaper were the "bits" which Mr Brown remembers buying as a child. *"We used to get a pen'orth of chips and two pennyworth of 'bits'. They were the tail ends of the fish... along with the chips, they used to feed six of us"*.

York's confectionery shop in Wharf Street (Mrs M Rudkin)

A SWEET TOOTH

Some of the most vivid memories of childhood around Wharf Street are of local sweetshops, and the Italian ice cream sellers who had settled in Leicester from the 1890s onwards - Rossa's, Poli's, Massarella's, Altobell's, and Mancini's among them.

Poli's in Erskine Street *"used to compete with Massarella's right down the bottom of Wharf Street... Poli's ice cream was very, very good. We used to be able to go there and get a penny 'licker' - that was a sort of bowl shape on a stem, and they'd fill it and then you licked it off. You'd get your tongue right in the bottom. It were marvellous..."*. Massarella's ice cream was *"really something"*, said another, recalling the Sunday afternoon treat of a basin of ice cream with red syrup, bought from his cart just after the First World War for 3d. Rossa's ice cream was made in Bedford Street at around the same time. The company was founded in the 1890s by Ralph Rossa, whose first ice cream vans consisted of converted funeral hearses.

In the 1930s, one ice cream seller popularly known as "Raz" had a stand on Russell Square. He *"used to give the paperboys credit until Friday"*, recalls a former resident, who also remembers Massarella's carts being accidentally set alight one year during the traditional Bonfire Night celebrations. Others recall being sent *"down to Birstall Street, to Eric's, for ice cream. He used to make it in a shed in the side of the house... He would give us an enamel bowl and a shilling. You used to queue up for hours for this ice cream..."*. Henry Curtis of Gladstone Street sold his own ice cream from a barrow in the street, *"in a white straw hat and snow white apron"*, while another well-known manufacturer, George Cox, was to be found nearby in Erskine Street.

Ice cream was virtually unobtainable when the ingredients were rationed during World War II, and its eventual reappearance made it even more memorable. Mancini's was particularly popular with children attending the nearby Taylor Street and St. Matthew's schools. *"I used to love the banana and vanilla flavour - it was... oh, you can't describe it! Soft and creamy. It was really nice"*, recalls one. *"Very, very nice ice cream"*, Margaret Zientek remembers, *"and he was very good to the children... I was told that he once brought ice creams round to all the children at school"*.

Large-scale commercial ice cream manufacturers such as Walls and Lyons claimed a growing share of the market after the Second World War, but until then several of the shops in the Wharf Street area also made their own ice cream. Ernie White describes the process:

"On Saturdays we used to make our own ice cream. We used to make it with sterilised milk, ice cream powder, pour it into a drum similar to a butter paddle in the middle, and churn away... our old Dad used to have us turning that runny stuff till it was absolutely full, because the more you turned it, obviously the more it made... we sold most of it in hap'orths and pen'orths on a little glass dish...".

Sweets were very popular with children, of course, and deciding what to buy was all part of the pleasure. *"Amongst the little cottages in Upper George Street"*, Dorothy Rayson remembers, *"was a favourite shop - really the front room of a house - where the occasional halfpenny could be spent. The old man in the shop sat all day in his rocking chair beside a fireplace with a mantle. On this stood jars of tobacco and snuff... Other shelves were filled with jars of sweets - Gobstoppers, Lovers' Lips, Kali Dabs, Humbugs and Wine Gums. It often took ages to make the mind up what to buy, but the old man never minded... There were lots of other shops in the area, but that had a certain charm of its own, especially to a child".*

Toffee apples were also a popular choice, but *"there was a herbalist in Willow Street..."*, one woman remembers, *"and we used to get this revolting stuff called liquorice root - you can actually still buy it in herbal shops... Horrible, revolting, all stringy - we loved it!"*. She also remembers another shop *"which I thought was lovely... I was about eight or nine years old... where they sold pink and white sugar mice. I used to stand with my nose pressed against the window!"*.

At Christmas the mice were joined in the window by sugar pigs and Santa Clauses. There were several confectionery shops in the area - "Muggy" Measures', Gorman's and York's in Wharf Street, and Jobling's on Humberstone Gate - but most corner shops sold sweets. At White's in Brook Street *"we'd make up halfpenny lucky bags for the kids. Sweets in those days were four ounces for twopence, and most people only spent either a halfpenny or a penny, so to give a kid four ounces for a halfpenny was quite a thing".*

STREET SELLERS

Despite the large number of shops in the area, street sellers were a familiar sight around Wharf Street before the Second World War. Several of them are recalled here by Mr Brown.

Today we have a population of mixed nationalities, but in the 1920s and 1930s, if we saw one Indian, it was a great surprise. I remember seeing one about once a year, a Sikh I believe, very tall, dark and what I remember best of all was the way he spoke in broken English while trying to sell his towels and handkerchiefs to customers.

Then there was the salt man. He had a small hand cart, loaded with huge blocks of salt, and he used to use a handsaw to cut off the amount you needed. This had to last until you saw him again, which was a three to four weeks wait.

There was the knife grinder with his homemade 'machine', which was a wooden frame, a cycle wheel (used to push it along), and a belt from the wheel to the sharpening stone. When he used to sharpen knives and scissors, he turned the whole frame upside down, and one of the bars was used as a treadle to operate the wheel and stone. I remember his shout of 'Grindo' when he was in the district....

The milkman also used a hand cart for a time, with a churn of milk in the centre. The milk was measured out in half pint or one pint jugs... The 'fruit and veg' man also had a long hand cart, loaded high with a large variety of fruit and vegetables, and his scales were sometimes a bit out of true. There were no inspectors then!

From the coalman with his horse and cart you could get 'cobbles', 'lumps', 'nutty slack', or his 'best', which was dearer than the others, but put out more heat. I also remember the newspaper man, whose cry of 'Papers!' used to echo all around, with his bundle of papers under his arm. Any time there was an 'emergency' or other special news, the papers were hurried through and on the street in a very short time".

Eldorado's ice cream cart in Crafton Street (Leicester City Council)

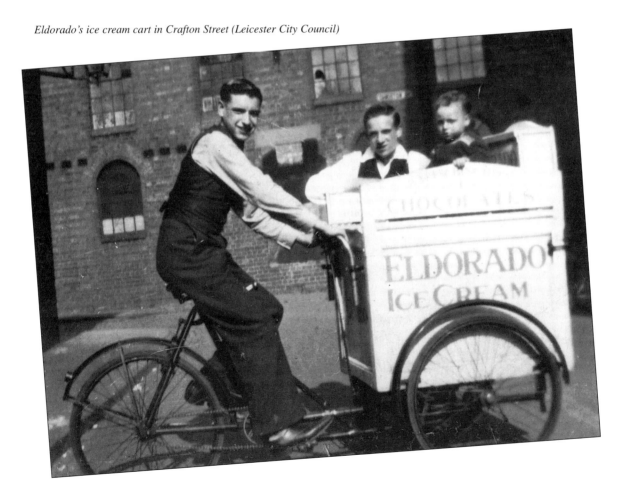

MAKING ENDS MEET

In 1936 a League of Nations report described Leicester as the most prosperous city in the British Empire, and the second most prosperous community in the world after The Hague. Its wide range of industries and high proportion of working women certainly protected it from the worst effects of the inter-war depression. Nevertheless, this judgement was based on such factors as the average level of household incomes, and like all averages, it concealed massive variations between the richest and poorest sections of the population.

SOME OF THEM WERE ATROCIOUSLY POOR

In the 1930s, low wages, irregular work and large family size all contributed to poverty, but the two main factors were the incapacity or absence of the main breadwinner - through illness, old age, death or desertion - and unemployment. Periods of short time work were always a feature of the local hosiery and footwear industries, but unemployment in the city rarely fell below 10,000 until the outbreak of war in 1939.

Unemployment relief - the "dole" - was subject to means testing, and applicants could also be refused if they failed to demonstrate that they were "genuinely seeking work". Many women were not covered by unemployment and sickness insurance schemes, and failed to qualify for any benefits at all. And as the Pilgrim Trust pointed out in 1938, unemployment in Leicester was all the more acutely felt *"for the contrast between the general prosperity, and the man or the family, who is standing outside it, but witnessing it all day and every day"*.

Much time, effort and money was spent by charitable bodies on alleviating poverty in the Wharf Street area, and these are more fully described elsewhere. It will also be evident from other sections of this book how much people relied on family and friends for help - in looking after children, for example, or during periods of illness. In the 1920s and 30s, however, the extreme poverty of some families in the Wharf Street area was only too obvious.

"It was a usual thing round about there to always see an awful lot of children...", said one former resident: *"in the winter they didn't have coats. They didn't even have shoes, 'cos I remember them coming to school like it, and they'd rub them - it was an old, old thing - they used to rub them with goose grease, and soak brown paper in goose grease and put it all round them, and an old jumper on top, and that's how they stayed the whole winter. And the children smelt because they'd got this*

goose grease on... some of them there were really, really atrociously poor...". Another said:

> *"Thinking about it now, when I went to school, children were ragged, they was sort of penalised, some of the children were. Everybody seemed to take it out on them, some of the teachers did, but.... it wasn't the children's fault, I mean, it was awful for them. But I can remember seeing boys with their trousers all bare bottoms, and little boots that were all wore down, elbows out of their jumpers, in school... I had friends who lived further down, and they were really poverty-stricken. You'd go in the houses, and it was just the bare bricks on the floor and newspaper on the tables...".*

Most children had to make do with clothes handed down from older brothers or sisters, bought second hand, or provided by local charities. Money was *"very scarce"*, wrote Mr Brown, *"and I remember my Dad had to walk to Friday Street to get a 'Distress' ticket, which paid so much for rent and food"*. Friday Street was the depot from which some of the unemployed were engaged on public works by the Council's Distress Committee - but *"most of our clothes came from the charity organisation, as did our school wear, shoes and clothes"*. Many children were provided with boots through a police charity, *"a great pair of clodhoppers with the letter 'L' on for all to see..."*, Dorothy Rayson recalls, *"to prevent them being pawned"*.

POP SHOPS... AND TICK

Children from better off families might have a new set of clothes once a year, usually bought for the annual Sunday School anniversary or a similar event to replace last year's "Sunday best". This was one reason why such occasions were so eagerly awaited. However, on Monday morning clothes new and old were likely to be among the items taken to the local pawn shop - either to Leif's at 27 Wharf Street, next door to the Hippodrome, or to Palfreyman's in Russell Square. Both had other pawnshops in working class districts of the city.

"Every Monday, sheets off the bed, our Sunday clothes would go to the pawn shop, and were brought out again on Saturday", Mr Brown recalls. Suits, dresses, and wedding rings were also commonly pawned, and even furniture would be "hocked" at times, with the pawnbroker coming round to padlock the room to make sure it was not used. *"Then of course... there was Leif's pawn shop"*, remembers Mrs Pettitt, who lived in Gladstone Street as a child:

> *"We used to go there every Monday morning, back again every Friday night. Washed, ironed Sunday, back again Monday. My Mam used to take FOR people in the street, them that was a little bit too 'posh', shall we say, and they daren't go themselves, so my Mam used to take the bundles for them 'cos she'd got twopence or threepence for doing it. They might have been poor, but they had their pride. False pride, I suppose... yes, there was quite a lot of that".*

Goods were redeemed at the end of the week once wages had been paid, but the few shillings the pawnbroker paid were an essential part of the family's income, and most found it impossible to escape the recurring cycle of debt in which they were trapped. The same was true of other forms of credit, like the "tick" extended by local shopkeepers. *"There was one lady..."*, remembers a former shopkeeper:

This building used to be Leif's pawnshop in Wharf Street. The Hippodrome cinema was on its right (Leicester City Council)

"we used to allow her credit, but every Friday that money was there. She never, ever let me down. Well, when they were going, moving them out to the estates, she said 'What am I going to do...?' 'Well, I said, you can still have your credit'. And her boy used to come from school at four o'clock every afternoon, fetch her groceries, and carry them back to Braunstone. And my money was there every Friday, he'd come down with the money. When we was going to retire, he said 'What am I going to do?'... so my husband said 'I'll tell you what you're going to do. You're not going to pay for this week's green groceries, groceries. Tell your mum she's got her money now to start paying where she is...".

Customers who did not pay could pose problems for shops already operating within low profit margins. *"Of course, having a little shop in an area of terraced houses, everybody knew everybody's problems..."*, said Ernie White:

"And then when it got to holiday times, when it got to Easter, Whit, Christmas or the week's holiday they used to have in August, people didn't get paid, so they invariably couldn't pay you, and we used to have to say... 'Don't worry about that money... we'll put that on the back of the book. Pay it off so much a week'. Well, by the time they'd paid off at about two bob (2s or 10p) a week, there was another holiday upon them, so consequently there was this amount of money with quite a lot of customers owing it in the back of the book, and I'm sure we had lots and lots of money owed to us".

49

As well as extending credit, shopkeepers could also help by selling goods in small quantities. *"In some ways he was a little bit of a soft touch"*, Ernie said of his father: *"You could tell him a bit of a sob story and he'd stand for it, then they wouldn't pay him, but somehow or other he got through. He would sell them ha'porths and pen'orths; sell them a pen'orth of sugar and a pen'orth of milk, cut a loaf of bread in half where other shops wouldn't do that...".*

Having goods "on tick" might be very common, but as Ernie Martin pointed out, there was still *"a stigma. If you had lots of stuff 'on tick', it was a sort of 'they owe a lot of money' sort of business, you know"*. Several shops operated hire purchase schemes, including Marvin's and Holyland's, *"where you could buy a wooden roller mangle for a shilling (5p) a week"*. An alternative was to pay small weekly sums into a "clothing club". *"My mother used to pay - I think it was the Prudential, I'm not sure what it was"*, Ernie remembers, *"but I know this man used to come round every Monday for two shillings... you paid two shillings for 20 weeks and you got an extra two shillings, and that used to buy me a pair of shoes, or my mother's shoes, or something else like that. I can see this man coming now...".* Marvin's operated a similar scheme, Harry Limbert recalls, and *"for as little as 3s. (15p) a week, you could get rigged out completely. All you had to do was obtain a ticket from an agent for anything from £1 upwards. A £3 ticket cost 3s a week for 21 weeks, and all Marvin's had to do was to serve you with what goods you wanted until the money had been spent. When I was about six my eldest brother, who was 14 years older than me, had a £3 ticket, and he took me with him to Marvin's and bought me my first snake belt, which cost sixpence halfpenny".*

MAKING A FEW COPPERS

Payments to "Christmas clubs" were another way of saving against future expenditure, but like the clothing "tickets" these were usually restricted to people able to pay a certain sum on a regular basis. Having a regular income, however small, made it easier to budget, but families whose members were unemployed, on short time work or bringing up children on their own often did not know from one week to the next what money they would have.

Every penny counted in these circumstances, and every member of the family of an age to do so was expected to contribute. Women with children often did outdoor work for local companies, enabling them to work at home. As one woman recalled as a child, *"my mother worked for Hart and Levy... and we used to take this work to Wimbledon Street on prams because it was outdoor work. And it was the only way she was able to bring us up... She'd be up sewing till twelve o'clock at night, be up again at four o'clock in the morning. She knew what hard work was".*

"I mean, me Mum had to do work", another remembers: *"She went out scrubbing to get money for buying dinners, you know, and this neighbour used to look after me till I went to school, or in the holidays. They were very good...".* Taking in washing was another way of earning a shilling or two. *"If you could afford it, you could pay people about half a crown (12.5p) to do your washing and ironing, usually older women with no pensions. Women often took in washing to make some money. You'd have the mangle in the scullery and washing hanging around everywhere to dry".*

Small sums of money could also be had from "rag and bone" merchants in the area, who came round with their horse-drawn carts, and *"would accept any old junk, and give the donor a few pennies in exchange..."*. One Wharf Street character mentioned by many people was the rag and bone man Arky Bennett, remembered for his repartee as well as the cups and saucers he gave for rags - *"a bit vulgar, but better than going to the pictures!"*. The waste merchants Cemmell's, which started in the area, were particularly popular with children because they exchanged unwanted items for goldfish. The other place *"to gain something from rubbish"*, Dorothy Rayson recalls, was the local chip shop - *"although this was 'kind' rather than cash... The 'chippy' was always glad of a few Daily Heralds to wrap up his goods, and his gratitude earned a full extra portion of chips"*.

Children were usually well aware of the family's financial situation, and did their bit to help out. *"To earn some money"* Pat Chapman remembers:

> *"boys went to the market to get some wooden boxes to chop into firewood, to go around the houses to sell. The girls ran errands and took babies in their prams for walks. We took rags and empty clean jam jars to Lees the rag merchants to earn money for going to the pictures... I worried about my Mum's difficulty about her shortage of money, so I wouldn't ask her for money for school outings and so on. I gave her my paper round money. I suppose in some ways we grew up in these things quickly"*.

Fetching coal in iron barrows from the merchant or the coal wharf on Humberstone Road was another way of earning a penny or two - *"hard work, half a hundredweight or more at a time, but if you didn't do it, you didn't get your money for the pictures"*. "Gratering" could also yield a profit, though this depended on being lucky enough to spot the objects of the exercise! *"You had a long piece of bamboo cane, with a slit in the end with a matchstick in it"*, explained one man, and *"you used this to grip coins which had fallen down gratings - you knocked the matchstick out and caught the coin between the cane"*. Other people used a knob of soap on the end of the stick to trap the coins.

Ernie Martin remembers making a modest profit from selling stales cakes at school. *"Along the Humberstone Road there was Poole's the caterers and cake shop. And in a morning I used to go in there and ask for 'a pennyworth of stales, please'... Used to take them to school and sell 'em! Not all of them... halfpenny each, something like that"*.

BREAD AND LARD

Along with ice cream, "stales" added a bit of variety to the staple diet, which was otherwise quite modest and predictable. "We did well if we got bread and jam for a meal", Mr Brown recalls, "and butter and sugar were a miracle. I can honestly say I was brought up on bread and lard, and still enjoy it even now". However, there were occasional other treats.

Ernie White's father used to buy specked oranges and apples from the wholesale market:

"probably a case of 300 oranges. You'd be lucky if you got fifty out of it any good, but if you've only paid a couple of bob, half a crown (12.5p) for it, so what! You could sell the wooden orange box for sixpence or ninepence (2.5 - 3.5p) as a rabbit hutch, and the rest of the oranges, you picked out the best. We cut the specks out, and kids used to come into the shop and buy specked oranges or specked apples that they could have on the way to school".

Rabbit was a cheap source of meat, and a regular feature of many people's diet. *"One shilling and sixpence for a rabbit, and they'd give you fourpence back for the skin. They'd say 'Do you want the skin?', and we used to make fur collars out of it..".* However, as Ernie White recalls, *"people wouldn't buy a rabbit if it was chopped up. Very few people would take that - no way! Because the idea was, you didn't know if it's tomcat or not!".* On Fridays, Ernie also recalls:

"We used to cook faggots, we used to sell faggots at two for three halfpence or a penny each... I know we had some faggots dropped on us one day that, they hadn't got what they called the sheep's skirt on them - they used to call them bales - whereas the sheep's skirt spread over the top of the faggot, which made them like a suet, made them more moist, more palatable, and we had some one day that didn't have this on, and people said 'No, we like faggots with bales on!' And we also used to do mushy peas, hot pig's belly, black pudding, all this sort of thing we sold on a Friday".

Cheap cuts of meat could provide a substantial meal with the addition of vegetables or dumplings, and in the days before fridges even the more expensive cuts be bought cheaply from butchers on Saturday evenings and Sundays. Very little was wasted. *"They say to you now, don't they, don't eat an egg that's cracked"*, said one woman, but *"we lived on cracked Egyptian eggs. My Mother used to go and buy them from Worthington's in Wharf Street, and there'd be egg shells floating. We had some lovely custards...".*

MATTERS OF LIFE AND DEATH

The welfare reforms of the 1940s, with their emphasis on a minimum standard of "social security", did not eliminate poverty - but they went some way towards alleviating its worst effects. The National Health Service, established in 1948, was one of the most significant in this respect, for as the Medical Officer of Health Dr Killick Millard noted in 1908, *"the general effect of poverty on physical health and efficiency is unmistakably bad..."*. In the early 1930s, death rates among the lowest income groups throughout the country were far higher than those among the wealthiest sections of the population. In Leicester itself in 1929, the death rate in the Wyggeston ward, which included most of the Wharf Street area, was almost 20 per 1000. In the middle class ward of Knighton it was less than 10:1000. In Wyggeston, 112 in every 1000 babies died before reaching the age of one; in Knighton, only 21:1000.

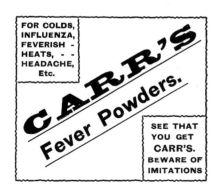

1907 advert for Carr's Fever Powders (Leicester City Council)

ASK FOR CARR'S... AND TAKE NO OTHER!

Damp and overcrowded housing, a limited diet and inadequate clothing all contributed to poor health, but illness was itself a major cause of poverty. Those too ill to work usually found their income drastically reduced, as did those forced to give up work to look after sick relatives - and the poorer the family, the less able it was to afford medical care when it needed it.

Before the National Health Service was established, *"people didn't go running off to the doctor every five minutes, because you had to be a member of a Friendly Society or something like that"*. Home remedies were usually the first resort for minor ailments: bread poultices were used for boils; goose grease or camphorated oil for a bad chest; a mustard foot bath for colds; oil of cloves for toothache. Butter was rubbed on bumps, and vinegar dabbed on the forehead for headaches. A weekly dose of syrup of figs, senna or similar was common *"to keep you regular"*, or as a "cure" for all manner of ailments: *"There was one old lady... and my husband always used to say, 'Don't ever tell Mrs X I'm ill - she'll always come across with the castor oil!'..."*.

Cheap patent medicines bought from local chemists were also commonly used, and the Wharf Street area was always well provided with such establishments. In 1899 James Morris of 33 Wharf Street was advertising his liver pills as *"the world's best remedy for all those evils which flow from a torpid or sluggish condition of the Liver"*, sold in boxes at $7^1/2^d$ and $1/11^1/2^d$ - or *"Post free, $8^1/2^d$ and $1/3^d$"*. In the same year, Samuel Cleaver of Wharf Street and Gladstone Street, was offering Cleaver's Cough Pills at a similar price, which *"if taken when the COLD COMMENCES, its advance is arrested, and the attack is repulsed without the slightest injury to the most delicate constitution of either sex... We assert within the pale of truth that if there is one Remedy in the World for COUGHS and their causes, COLDS, CHEST COMPLAINTS and LUNG DISEASES, that Remedy is... CLEAVER'S COUGH PILLS"*.

However, even Cleaver's remedies never achieved the popularity of Carr's Fever Powders, first produced in the later 19th century by William Carr on his premises at 7 Upper George Street, before the family business moved to a larger site at 170 (later 168) Wharf Street. *"Beneficial alike for Children and Adults"*, claimed an advert in 1888, *"The best and safest Medicine for Colds, Feverish Heats, Sore Throats, Loss of Appetite, Lowness of Spirits, Headache, Measles, Scarletina, etc., etc.... The ever-increasing sale of these Powders proves their value... Ask for CARR'S Powders, and take no other"*.

To guard against "chills", some children were regularly given a fever powder after having a bath, *"whether you needed it or not"*. Some of the recipients of Carr's fever powders were none too enthusiastic about them, however! *"They came in white paper packets"*, recalls one:

> *"and when you opened it up there was a sort of horrible dark, purply looking stuff... If you were feeling ill, it's the last thing in the world you wanted to take! It tasted horrible! I'll never forget, because at that time I had a goldfish, and my Mother had said to me 'if you get wet, you'll catch a cold!'. So you'd got to take a Carr's fever powder. So I looked at the goldfish in the bowl, and I thought - 'This poor goldfish is ever so wet, so I'll have to give it Carr's fever powder'! Unfortunately the fish had a watery grave..."*.

Next door to Carr's, on the corner of Wharf Street and Upper George Street, was Beaumont's drug store. Harry Limbert, whose wife once worked there, understands that Mr Beaumont *"tried to buy the formula, but the old chap refused to sell and shortly afterwards died, taking it with him"*. One woman who lived in the area as a child remembers that Beaumont's had *"all the wooden drawers with the little pot handles... these great big apothecary's bottles and jars filled with liquid, and we used to think it was a treat to go and look at this. They sold everything...."*. It was from

Beaumont's, someone else recalls, that *"I bought my first Tangee lipstick... I had nowhere to keep it, because you weren't allowed private places at home, so I used to walk round with it up my breeches leg till it melted away!"*.

In the 1920s, Martin's chemist's also had a shop in Willow Bridge Street. Mr Martin, writes Harry Limbert, *"made his own baby food, a long time before 'Cow and Gate' came on the market. My parents lived at the bottom of Syston Street near the Plumbers' Arms, and that's where the first half of their ten children were born. They were all fed on Martin's home-made baby food... My old Dad told me that Mr Martin wanted to take a photo of the family to advertise his baby food, but I never saw one"*.

By the 1930s a whole range of mass-produced patent medicines were available for sale in general stores. *"We used to have cards and cards of pills"*, Ernie White remembers:

"various types of pills made by various firms... penny or twopence a box - there'd be things like back and kidney, liver and kidney... pills which were supposed to be suitable for ladies who had got themselves into some sort of situation... and I remember people coming in and buying half a dozen tins of Penny Royal at a time if they thought they were like that - you know, pregnant. Whether they ever did any good, I did ask one of these travellers on one occasion... he said 'All these various things, they all come out the same machine... we colour them a bit different, put them in different boxes'... There was a tremendous trade in just these odds and ends. Things like Indian brandy... which used to sell at threepence an ounce, and they'd bring in a little bottle... that was supposed to cure stomach upsets and all that sort of thing. And we used to sell Butler's, a well known old manufacturing chemist in Leicester. They used to sell a sort of liver salt called a Sea Breeze, and they used to say 'Our Sea Breeze will keep you moving'. It certainly did if you took too much!"

THE CLINIC

Access to a doctor for more serious illnesses was largely limited by the ability to pay. Medical care was available under the Poor Law for the destitute, but "a trip to the 'parish' for a free pass" was a last resort because of the stigma attached to claiming any form of poor relief - one which lingered on for some time after the Poor Law itself was abolished in 1930. In the early 20th century, the Ragged School Mission in Bedford Street also had a "Healing Night" every Wednesday for those unable to afford a doctor, and "this must have given comfort, if not actual healing".

For those with regular work and relatively high wages - always a minority - the services of a doctor could be obtained through the Leicester Public Medical Service. This originated from the Leicester Provident Dispensary, which was established in East Bond Street in the 1830s, and had a branch dispensary in Chester Street, near to St. Matthew's church. Its main purpose was to provide medical and dental care for those covered by the 1911 National Insurance Act - also a minority - and its doctors were often referred to as "Lloyd Georges" after the architect of the Act, the Liberal Chancellor of the Exchequer David Lloyd George.

However, the Public Medical Service also catered for uninsured people, who were able to obtain medical attendance in exchange for weekly payments of 6d - 1s. *"If you went to work"* as Elsie Hodgson explained, *"you got a National Health doctor, a 'Lloyd George' they called it then, and my mother, she belonged to a doctor's club. She didn't work, you see, and she had to pay a shilling a week for herself, and sixpence a week for each of us kids until we started work, then we paid our own 'Lloyd George', because we started work at 14"*.

The Chester Street Dispensary - or "the Clinic", as it was known locally - was familiar ground to many local children, who were regularly sent to pick up family prescriptions. For many years it also housed a Minor Ailments Clinic run by the Leicester School Medical Service. *"Say the School Nurse decided you'd got a rash and you needed something on it..."*, said Elsie, *"or you had a cut and you needed stitching, she sent you to the nearest dispensary, you see. Also I had to fiddle down the Dispensary for my Mum if she'd had the doctor, and so I spent an awful lot of time round there!"*.

Around the time of the Second World War, remembers Margaret Zientek (nee Barrass), a teacher at St. Matthew's school, all the children *"had a green Clinic card they'd carry to school with them, so if they had a scab on them, or they cut themselves or anything, or they weren't well, you sent them round the clinic to see Nurse Burden... she was there for years and years... and she used to go round to the schools, also examine heads and bodies, and hands..."*.

Children found to have lice or scabies were also sent to the Clinic. *"The Nurse came to check heads... and looked in between our fingers..."*, said one: *"Every summer we had heat bumps, but I know now they must have been flea bites. Nearly every child had lice, if only mildly. It was inevitable. My Mum used to toothcomb my hair most nights... I hated it. I never had a note from the 'nit nurse', though"*. Ringworm, a fungus infection, was also very common, and much to the horror of the children themselves - who were teased and shunned at school - was commonly treated with telltale applications of Gentian Violet: *"blue unction - a cure for everything!"*.

THE NEIGHBOURS RALLIED ROUND

In 1929 - a fairly typical year - the Wyggeston ward had the highest tuberculosis rate in the city, and the highest rate of illness from other infectious diseases. Before antibiotics became available, there was little effective treatment for such illnesses apart from isolation, good food and rest and - in the case of TB - fresh air.

As Ernie White pointed out, *"there was no cure for TB then. They would cart people up to Groby Road Hospital... my sister had TB in October 1938 and had died by June 1939. People were afraid of TB..."*. The illness placed a heavy burden on other members of the family, who could quickly find themselves unemployed if they took time off to care for relatives. Dorothy Rayson recalls that one woman, who lived in a cottage belonging to the Ragged School Mission:

"was in the last stages of consumption... and because her husband was fortunate enough to be in work, he dared not take time off to look after her for fear of losing his job. All the neighbours rallied round. On sunny days they would push her bed outside to give her a breath of air. On cold days, coal would be found from somewhere to light a fire. All through the long days the lady had a stream of visitors, making tea, nursing her, keeping her company, and this continued until she died".

This sort of help was also crucial for women expecting a baby. The Public Medical Service provided midwives for subscribers and also operated a small maternity hospital in Bond Street - but again, this was not an option open to everyone. The rules of the Royal Infirmary, a charitable institution until 1948, prevented it from admitting any but "complicated" pregnancies, and the maternity service provided by the North Evington Poor Law Infirmary met with the same resistance as other Poor Law services, even when it was taken over by the Borough Council in 1930 as the

Tuberculosis wards at Groby Road Hospital (Leicester City Council)

City General Hospital. As Ernie White noted: *"the Royal Infirmary was kept going by voluntary contributions. But people used to be very proud to say they'd had an operation in the Royal, because the City General... for many, many years, was known as the Poor Law institution. People looked upon it as a glorified workhouse..".*

In the 1920s and 1930s, most women would call instead on the services of the local "handywoman", indispensable at both extremes of life in exchange for a small fee or payment in kind. *"In Gladstone Street"*, Mrs Pettitt remembers, *"there was a lady called Mrs Tate. Now she did laying out and bringing forth! I think she did a lot round the area. I can always remember her because she was quite a big person, and she always used to wear a snow-white apron".* The birth rate in the Wyggeston ward was among the highest in the city. Given the option, many men as well as women would have chosen to have fewer children, but free advice about birth control was difficult to come by before World War II. Government regulations prevented local authorities from offering it until 1930, and even then it was limited to married women who had a medical condition.

Groby Road, the City General and the Infirmary were all taken over by the National Health Service in 1948, but even then, recalls Iris Smith who had her first baby in 1953, *"you had a job to go away to have a child. Because we'd got our own bedroom, I had to have him at home. No choice. But I think a lot depended on your doctor, and my doctor was in favour of home births".*

A DECENT FUNERAL

The stigma attached to the Workhouse and the fear of the "pauper's funeral" are still strong in the popular memory, and even now elderly people will make great sacrifices to ensure they leave enough money for a "decent" funeral. After the First World War, when unemployment benefits were limited to just a few "precarious" trades, and only the relatively well-off could afford subscriptions to Friendly Societies or burial clubs, working class families relied once again on friends and neighbours for help at such times.

House-to-house collections were held to help pay for the funeral, or money raised in other ways. One woman recalls, as a child during World War I, paying a penny to see the body of another child killed in an accident. The family *"had him in the front room in a little coffin... I suppose they needed the money to bury him... Most of the children went...".*

Until after World War II, it was usual for bodies to lie at home in the coffin until the funeral - in the parlour of the larger houses, or in the living room of "two up, two down" houses, and of shops which had only one room and a kitchen downstairs. It was also the custom to keep a light in the room overnight, *"so the corpse shouldn't be left alone in the dark"* - or perhaps so the living should not be frightened by stumbling across a coffin in the dark.

It was usual to wear black for the funeral, and for some time afterwards if the deceased was a close relative, but few people could afford new clothes on such occasions. They could have suits dyed at local laundries - both the Wyvern and Willow laundries had branches in the area - or if that was beyond their means, show the necessary respect by wearing a black armband. Black boards were often nailed across the window to denote a death in the house, *"a sort of four inch board put up the side of the window... and it was the custom in those days that when the funeral took place, everyone in the street drew their curtains, and you would have quite a little gathering of people outside the door to see the cortege move off".*

The "local" undertaker for much of the area was George Stanion, whose business was based in Alma Cottages at 155 Brunswick Street, near St. Matthew's Infants' School. However, it was usually the "handywoman" who laid out the dead. *"In our particular area"*, recalls Ernie White, *"there was a lady that was noted for laying out people and doing a good job... And she would send her two lads round to borrow the shutters. We used to put shutters up at the shop windows...".* Collections were still held once state benefits became more widely available after the Second World War. *"When anyone died"*, Ernie continues:

"they used to have collections down the street. They would come down with a list, knock the door, and they would say 'Well, we're collecting for old Charlie', or something like that. And the money they collected, they would go and buy a wreath, and that would be hung on our shop at the bottom of the Stocking Entry, because we were about halfway... they would hang the wreath up outside with a card on, 'In loving memory from all the neighbours', and if there was any money left they usually gave it to the widow or widower..."

Most funerals were modest affairs, but the "do" afterwards could be the occasion for a bit of showing off among neighbours. *They used to really 'swank' on what they buried the old man with...*", says Ernie:

"You'd probably have a couple of ladies in the shop, and one would say... 'Tell 'em, Ern, what we had', and I'd say 'Well, you had two pound of ham'... 'Yes, but we didn't have that cheap shoulder ham, we had the best gammon ham, didn't we? You tell 'em... We had cream cakes...'. I mean, this was normal conversation, how people used to talk".

Old clothes could be dyed for a funeral at a local laundry (Leicester City Council)

BEST AND BUSIEST.

☞ Send Post Card To-Day for Van to Call.

Nat. Tel.
174X.

WYVERN

Nat. Tel.
174X.

Sanitary Laundry

LIMITED,

BELGRAVE, LEICESTER,

Shirt and Collar Dressers,

Dyers and Cleaners.

BEST FOR COLOUR AND FINISH.

Vans call on you direct, or Parcels may be left at
Receiving Offices :

4, Tudor Road,

38, Braunstone Gate,

10, Wharf Street,

48, Belgrave Road,

8, Sparkenhoe Street,

183, Charnwood Street.

Send Post Card To-Day for Van to Call.

In the garden of the Ragged School Mission (left to right) Audrey Hearn, Dorothy Rayson, Elsie Moore, Mary Selvedge (baby), Joyce Selvedge, Jennifer Rayson (front) and Alma Payne. (Mrs D Rayson)

RAGGED SCHOOL MISSION

The first Ragged Schools, for the education of destitute children, were founded by John Pounds, a Portsmouth shoemaker, around 1818. However, the movement really became established in the 1840s, under the patronage of Lord Ashley, 7th Earl of Shaftesbury, to cater for the innumerable children to be found on the streets of English towns and cities. The Leicester Ragged School Mission on the corner of Bedford Street and George Street was one of the most important sources of charitable aid in the Wharf Street area.

PLEAD THE CAUSE OF THE POOR AND NEEDY

This account of the Mission's history has been contributed by Mr William Pyne, whose father Will and mother Lucy were for many years caretakers at the Mission. Will Pyne was formerly a Regimental Sergeant Major in the Leicestershire Regiment, and served for some time in India.

In December 1866, Miss Fanny Wheeler, youngest daughter of a local manufacturer, invited into her home in Belgrave Gate on Sunday afternoons, boys and girls who at that time lived on the streets, neglected and uncared for. Thus began the work of the Leicester Ragged School Mission. As a tribute to its success, some of her earliest scholars - now respectable citizens - attended her funeral in 1909. Even today, around the world, there is still a fair number of an older generation who remember with deep affection the work of the Mission over a period of 80 years.

The work begun by Fanny Wheeler expanded rapidly. Aimed directly at the most deprived social outcasts, unwashed, half-starved and totally illiterate, it challenged head-on the ghastly poverty of the times. After a series of moves from Belgrave Gate, with 69 scholars and seven teachers, it moved in 1872 to the old Gladstone Music Hall, Wharf Street, on a seven year lease. By the end of that time, there were 370 Sunday School scholars and 200 day school pupils. The newly formed Leicester School Board took over the day school activities in 1871, but the Mission started a building fund, backed by Dr Barnardo who appealed for support, and eventually the site of the old Methodist Chapel in Bedford Street was acquired and building began. The Earl of

Shaftesbury became its first President and Patron, and there were now 564 Sunday scholars and 37 teachers. The new Mission Hall, opened in February 1885, began the famous Robin Breakfasts at Christmas that year.

Eleven years later, the Mission purchased adjoining property. Classrooms were extended, the School house rebuilt with a soup kitchen next door, and a grand public opening of the extension took place on 7 December 1896. There were now 859 scholars and 41 teachers - some of them former scholars whose natural intelligence had at last been given a chance to develop. A Visiting Sister, Miss Emma Hollington, was appointed in 1901, and for no fewer than 45 years served in that capacity, a familiar figure in the Wharf Street area.

Meanwhile, the Mission, affiliated to the Ragged School movement in London, was visited by Sir John and Lady Kirk, both national figures in the Shaftesbury Society, to open its first Sale of Work, an annual effort held in the wealthier part of the town which maintained the Mission's Benevolent Fund. It continued well into the 1930s.

The bitter years of the First World War failed to stop the work, but they took a fearful toll among the teachers and older pupils who were killed on active service - an experience tragically repeated in the Second World War. There were, however, always volunteers from the many to whom the Mission had been almost a home. The natural passing of founders from the more privileged classes left gaps which were filled by the very people they had sought to help. No better tribute to the sincerity and effectiveness of the Mission's purpose could be found.

Those who remember what life was like in the 1870s and 1880s have long since gone, but there are many who can still recall the Mission's continuing work between the Wars. Until the 1930s, the Bedford Street and Wharf Street areas were for the most part slums of the worst kind, and much of the work was perforce of a charitable nature. It was still necessary for its workers to hold firm to its original motto, a line from the Book of Proverbs: 'Plead the cause of the poor and needy'. Its workers did just that without any thought of reward.

SPIRITUAL WELFARE, PRACTICAL CARE

In the 1930s, when a storeroom was being cleared, a hand-written notice was found setting out "The Rules" of the Mission school in its early days:

1. No child will be barred through lack of suitable clothing.
2. Some cleanliness must be observed, and all attendees must have clean hands and faces, with hair neatly combed.
3. Shoes, if worn, must be wiped clean before entering the classroom.
4. Children must attend regularly. Bad behaviour will result in dismissal.
5. Slates and chalk must remain in the classroom.

However, as the Mission's own reports record, it was not always easy to persuade the children to attend. *"The influence of the Sunday School on the scholars is very marked"*, it was noted in 1886. *"Those who first came in rags and dirt are now clean and tidy. This very fact was found to act as a deterrent to other ragged street boys who manifest a decided dislike to entering an orderly respectable looking school. The teachers perceived that some special methods must be adapted..."*. The children were *"enticed with the promise of a piece of cake... In this way a school of from 70 to 80 boys and girls has been gathered, most of whom attend regularly"*. By 1914, however, it was noted that *"the numerous and increasing attractions for young people on Sunday in large towns like Leicester tends to seriously disturb the habit of regular attendance at Sunday School, making it impossible to maintain the higher level of former years"*.

Miss Fanny Wheeler, founder of the Leicester Ragged School Mission (Mr W Pyne)

The Mission enjoyed the support of some influential patrons. They included Henry Lawrence, an accountant; his brother Joseph, a master printer and founder of the firm Raithby Lawrence; and William Thornley, proprietor of the printing firm of W. Thornley in Bowling Green Street, Leicester, and the Mission's Treasurer for many years. Dorothy Rayson (nee Pyne), Will and Lucy's daughter, recalls that Henry Lawrence was Superintendent of the Boys' School until the 1930s, when he was well over 80 years old.

The Mission building was extended in the 1890s and a three-storey caretaker's house was also provided, connected to the Mission by a large yard. "It was a large house", Dorothy remembers:

"Upstairs there were four big bedrooms and a 'Blanket Room' filled from floor to ceiling with soft woollen blankets, carefully stored in paper and camphor mothballs. Downstairs the front room was kept for 'best' and only ever used at Christmas or very special occasions. The living room was the heart of the house, comfortable, homely and furnished with mismatched chairs, a table covered with green felt and cheerful rag rugs. The kitchen was huge, and designed to prepare the great variety of food for Mission functions. It was dominated by a coal-fed copper in one corner, a big stone sink with a cold water tap, and a double-sized gas cooker".

Sunday services and weekday evening classes for adults were also held at the Mission. In the later 19th century one of the most popular weekday meetings was the Band of Hope. Drink was cheap and easily obtainable, but excessive drinking was undeniably the cause of a great deal of poverty, neglect and misery, with wives and children often the main victims. Scientific experiments illustrating the effects of alcohol were one feature of temperance meetings at the Mission, along with dramatic renditions of anti-drink novels such as *The Actress's Daughter* and *The Little Lamplighter*. Most popular of all were the "Magic Lantern" shows, when one of the helpers recited such tales as *The Drunkard's Daughter* as the pictures were projected onto a white sheet pinned to the wall.

During the 1930s, the Magic Lantern, complete with glass slides and the full text of *The Drunkard's Daughter* was found in a store cupboard at the Mission. Dorothy recalls that *"we begged my father to set the contraption up for the entertainment of me and my friends. Being children used to the wonder of talking movies, we laughed at the poor 'Drunkard's Daughter' till our sides ached. My irate father put the Magic Lantern away, and it never saw the light of day again"*.

Spiritual welfare was its main aim, but the Ragged School Mission also offered practical help to the children and their families. As the Annual Report put it in 1886, *"No one, certainly, can teach long in a Ragged School without feeling pity for the helpless condition of many of the children. A soup kitchen was opened in December, and... teachers were able to provide soup*

(Above) Will Pyne, ex-RSM, caretaker of the Mission and (below) his wife Lucy (Mr W Pyne)

free several times a week... In addition, 'bread tickets' representing 242 loaves of bread have been given to needy families, and groceries also". The Mission also ran a Clothing Club, and a Penny Savings Bank, which in 1886 had 2010 subscribers and assets of £71 19s (£71.95p), which *"gives us reason to indulge in the hope that thrifty habits are steadily growing among the people"*.

By the earlier 20th century, as the Visiting Sister's reports show, the Mission's Benevolent Fund was providing all kinds of support to the poor and needy. *"There are old people, too, with no friends who can help them, and only the Old Age Pension of 5s. per week to live upon. A number of such we help regularly with little gifts of food, and in the winter, an occasional bag of coal - a gift that gives most delight..."*. Emma Hollington, popularly known as 'The Lady in Grey' came to the Mission at the beginning of the century, the only

salaried worker apart from the caretaker. *"Her official title was Visiting Sister"*, Dorothy writes:

"though she was to become much more than that to so many people... She was a tall, thin lady with a sharp face and hair tied back in a severe bun. Her uniform was to her own design: a neat grey dress with a snow-white collar and a little black velvet bonnet... Although she could be quite strict, sometimes she had a remarkably good sense of humour, which was perhaps essential considering some of the places she had to visit. Everyone recalls that she was extremely kind to the children in her care. Miss Hollington was certainly a special lady, and was connected with every aspect of Mission life: the treats, the weekday and Sunday meetings, the sick-visiting, the distribution of blankets and 'Robins' Breakfasts'. The list was endless, Miss Hollington tireless...".

"Ole Piney, as we kids affectionately knew him in the late 1920s, was no ordinary run-of-the-mill caretaker... Until the end of his life, he always ate a raw onion for his supper every night! He claimed it was to ward off a recurrence of the malaria he had contracted in India, and vowed that on route marches he preferred an onion to water! Surprisingly (considering his army background) he never swore, but he said 'Blinking' a lot, much to the annoyance of his wife".

Mr Len Wilkinson

Tireless indeed! The Mission's Annual Report for 1916 records that in the previous year alone, Miss Hollington made no less than 1,652 visits to families in the area. The Mission also loaned blankets to those families unable to afford to buy them. *"With the coming of autumn..."*, recalls Dorothy of the 1930s, *"out came the blankets from the 'Blanket Room' at the top of the house... and for an entire week the long washing lines in the Mission yard were filled with blankets being given an airing. Word soon got around. Either people could smell the camphor, or hear the flapping, for they were soon joining the queue to borrow the wonderful winter warmers. Lucy kept a neat record of all the borrowers in an exercise book... the blankets had to be returned by the end of March...".*

ANNIVERSARY SUNDAY

Popular events at the Mission in the 1920s and 30s included the Harvest Festival, when the large hall was decorated with sheaves of corn begged from the Horse Repository in Charles Street, and "everyone brought along something... even a single apple was welcome... and on Monday everything was donated to the poor of the community". Anniversary Sunday was also eagerly awaited, and "an air of excitement pervaded everywhere, for it was on this special Sunday too that prizes were handed out for regular attendance".

The entire Sunday School would practice special anthems and hymns, and the children would wear new clothes for the occasion - though with unexpected results in one instance. *"One family who regularly attended Sunday School was a large one"*, Dorothy remembers:

"There were five children, with both parents out of work. One of the girls had a sweet clear

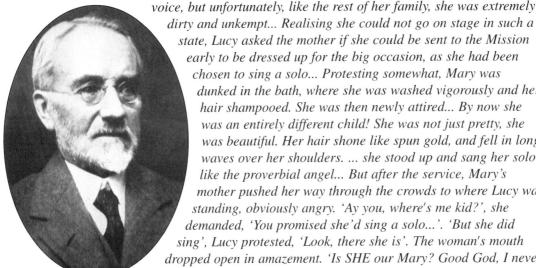

voice, but unfortunately, like the rest of her family, she was extremely dirty and unkempt... Realising she could not go on stage in such a state, Lucy asked the mother if she could be sent to the Mission early to be dressed up for the big occasion, as she had been chosen to sing a solo... Protesting somewhat, Mary was dunked in the bath, where she was washed vigorously and her hair shampooed. She was then newly attired... By now she was an entirely different child! She was not just pretty, she was beautiful. Her hair shone like spun gold, and fell in long waves over her shoulders. ... she stood up and sang her solo like the proverbial angel... But after the service, Mary's mother pushed her way through the crowds to where Lucy was standing, obviously angry. 'Ay you, where's me kid?', she demanded, 'You promised she'd sing a solo...'. 'But she did sing', Lucy protested, 'Look, there she is'. The woman's mouth dropped open in amazement. 'Is SHE our Mary? Good God, I never recognised me own daughter in that get-up!'. But on Monday morning all the nice clean clothes were taken to the pawn shop, never to be seen again"!

Henry Lawrence, Hon. Secretary
of the Mission for many years
(Mr W Pyne)

LAST YEARS OF THE MISSION

Dorothy recalls that *"it was a great struggle to keep the Mission functioning during the war, but some activities still continued. Of course, the Boys' Club dwindled, as only those too young to be called up were left. The Girls' Club flourished, however, and they put on several shows throughout the years. The old folk were the biggest concern, particularly through the cold winters".*

However, despite rationing, *"the Mission was still able to provide light refreshments for the old folk, who would come to the Mission for warmth and comfort. The Sunday School, too, kept going, and on occasions even an outing was possible. After the war it was hoped that resources for the Mission could be rebuilt... For a time this was a success, but it was uphill work".*

In the post-war period, full employment and welfare reforms went far to reduce the need for the charitable efforts of the Mission, but the biggest blow came from the re-housing schemes of the early 1950s, as those who had attended it were scattered far and wide across the city. It was finally closed on Sunday 25 April 1954, when *"for the last time, the Big Hall was packed with people who had come to say farewell. It was a tearful occasion for many... but it was right that the Mission should be given the dignity of closing in the appropriate way".*

In the following year, the building was sold to the local Association of Boys' Clubs, but competition from other leisure attractions in the 1950s eventually forced its closure, and the site was purchased by a private company for use as a car park. When the floor of the Big Hall was dug up, workmen were surprised to find graves underneath it, and several lurid theories circulated about their origins - that they were victims of the plague or mediaeval mass murder - until the press were reminded that this part of the Mission had been built on the site of the Methodist chapel.

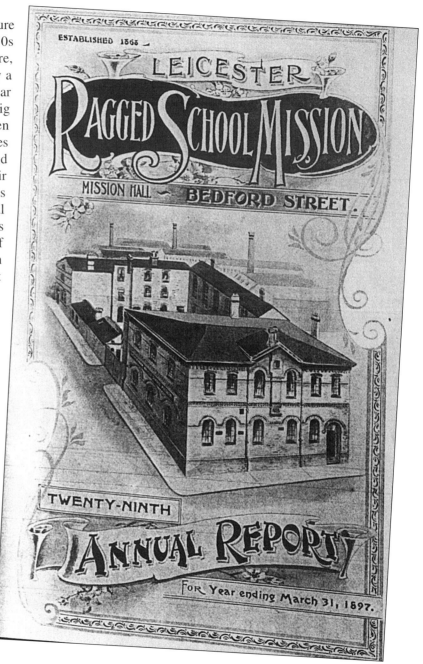

The Ragged School Mission on the corner of Bedford Street and George Street (Mr W Pyne)

Girls from Carley Street chapel with one of their teachers. From (L) to (R): Hazel Greet, Pat Boot, Pauline Sharpe, Miss Ivy Gray, Phyllis Bishop, Ivy Pritchard, Mary Creese (Mrs P Chapman)

CHURCHES AND CHAPELS

The spiritual welfare of the working classes was a matter of increasing concern in the early 19th century, as large numbers of people flocked to the towns, and relations between employers and workers were seen as becoming more distant and impersonal. This concern was heightened by the Religious Census of 1851, which suggested a serious decline in attendance at a place of worship. However, religious bodies played a central role in the life of the area. As well as campaigning against drink and other "evils", they dispensed charitable aid, and until the advent of Board Schools after 1870, their Sunday Schools and day schools were the main source of education for the children of the poor. In the 20th as well as the 19th century, they were also a focus of all kinds of social activities for children and adults alike.

CARLEY EVANGELICAL BAPTIST CHURCH

Carley Street Baptist Church is the oldest surviving religious establishment in the Wharf Street area. The eminent Baptist minister Robert Hall, of Harvey Lane Chapel in Leicester, was among those who preached at the opening of the chapel in June 1823.

Modest in size, but *"neat and comfortable... very pleasant to the occupants"*, it cost £170 to build and was designed by the local architect A.E. Sawday. Sixty children were soon enrolled in the Sunday School, but the congregation had little to spare in the way of money, and it was a constant task to raise enough to continue. Brother Gamble, it was noted in February 1825, had been *"out several weeks begging for the Chapel"*, while in December 1830 it was *"resolved that every member of this Church be required to pay the least 1d per week towards carrying forward the cause of Christ here"*.

The Church demanded strict standards of behaviour from its members, and excluded those who failed to meet them - using *"profane language"*, for example, and *"going to a Public House on the Lord's Day"*. In November 1852, *"Harriet B. having confessed that she had attended the races, she be suspended from our Communion"*, while two years later *"the name of Delilah H. be erased from the list of members. It is feared that her conduct agrees with her name"*. On the other hand, some were excused regular attendance because of the demands of work. Sister Cooper *"is unable to attend at the ordinance on Sabbath afternoons"*, it was noted in 1855, *"her husband being a cow-keeper and requiring her assistance"*.

For 17 years between 1843 - 60, the Rev. Joseph F. Winks was unpaid Minister at the Church. Described by his son as *"very Evangelical, highly doctrinal and often argumentative"*, he was a man of strong political convictions, and earlier served as a member of the reformed Borough Corporation. Before moving to Leicester he had a printing business in Loughborough in which he employed fellow

RODWELL'S MISSION

One of the more unusual religious institutions in the area, Rodwell's Mission in Crafton Street was commended by a history of Sunday Schools in Leicester in 1935 for "its success in premises of very limited accommodation, and for the brave way it carries on with practically no outside support". It was set up early this century by Francis "Dagger" Rodwell, a local chimney sweep, who "used to gather round him a number of poor boys, forming them into a band and helping them in various ways", using a small room at the back of his house at 83 Crafton Street as a Sunday School. Following his death, "his son and other devoted helpers carry on a gracious service. Each year the teachers and scholars do well in our Scripture Examination, and have gained the City Shield on more than one occasion".

Baptist and future travel pioneer Thomas Cook. He ran a similar business in High Street, Leicester, for some 40 years and wrote a number of pamphlets urging legal and constitutional reforms, *"one of which the authorities decided to confiscate, but he had prior warning of their plans... When they arrived they found on the shelves of his printing press several parcels neatly labelled with the title of the pamphlet. They hauled them off to the Town Hall, where they found they were all full of blank sheets and as they returned across the Market Place, found the real pamphlet selling furiously"*.

The Minister earned the nickname *"Red Herring Winks"* for this escapade, but he was also prominent in the campaign in the early 1830s to end the practice of gibbeting - one applied in 1832 to the body of the Leicester murderer James Cook after his execution at the Borough Gaol. Winks' campaign helped to arouse *"so vehement and articulate a revulsion"* among the public that the body was taken down and buried after three days, and the practice was prohibited soon afterwards by Parliament.

The Chartist leader and journalist Thomas Cooper, who had taught with Winks in the Gainsborough Adult Schools in Lincolnshire, and was active for some years in Leicester, was accepted into Carley Street Church. He was baptised at Friar Lane on 12 June 1859. Cooper, once a Methodist, had rejected all religion for some years before reaching *"a conviction of personal sin... I felt my old love for Methodism return; but I could not bring my mind to return to the old body of Methodists... reflection soon made me a Baptist in conviction, and on Whit Sunday, 1859, my old and dear friend Joseph Foulkes Winks immersed me in baptism..."*.

By the mid 1930s the church was beginning to be affected by the movement of population out of the area. *"Sunday School declining in number because of slum clearance"*, it was noted in 1938, and the church was also without a minister from February 1937, until the arrival of the Rev. P. J. Smith from Bradford in September 1941. After leaving Carley Street in 1947, Rev. Smith spent 24 years in London before entering a ministry in California, USA. He wrote recently of his *"happy six years as Pastor of the old Carley Street Baptist Church... It was quite a step of faith to accept their call to the Pastorate, as the work was in a very low state, but in the goodness of the Lord it soon built up as many were added to the normal population because Leicester was a fairly safe city. The Church became the meeting point for fine young people from various parts of the UK, including refugees from the Channel Islands..."*.

Mrs Dorothy Cope, who has attended Carley for over 50 years, recalls Rev. Smith as *"a keen young minister who had the spiritual welfare of the people in the area at heart... We held 'Open-Airs'... and had special Convention Meetings for young and old in the Church... So keen was the pastor to evangelise that he had a meeting for the 'drunks' at 11 pm on VE Day"*. Of the Open-air services in Humberstone Gate, she recalls, *"it was the norm to have hot dogs and fireworks thrown at us, but no one was ever put off from attending!"*.

The renewal of slum clearance in the 1950s meant the demolition of the old Carley Street chapel, and the building of a new one on a site in Wharf Street, at a cost of almost £27,000. However, such was the loyalty of its members that the movement of population out of the area did not affect it as much as might be anticipated. The congregation was never drawn exclusively from the Wharf Street area, but even those who moved elsewhere often continued to attend. *"My memories are of a very caring and lovely fellowship"*, writes one member, who started there in the 1920s at the age of three, and still attends. *"I knew them and liked them so much..."*, said another, who used to keep a shop in

Zion Chapel in Erskine Street (Leicester City Council)

Wharf Street,, *"I find it quite a long way now, but I can't give it up... you cannot believe how lovely these chapel people are.."*.

Pat Chapman remembers some of the regular weekday events at the chapel: the Sunshine Hour for children from the ages of 3-14, with hymns and slides about Bible stories; the Girls Club for 8-14 year olds; and the Covenanters' night for girls over 12 - *"painting, games, quizzes, singing, always finishing with a Bible story"*. The group was led by Miss Hill, Mrs Adams, Miss Gray and Miss Hunt, who were *"very patient with us, as we were quite rowdy. We went on public transport on summer evenings to Groby and Bradgate, and swimming on rare occasions"*.

For Pat and others, Carley had a lasting influence on their lives. *"I am still in touch with individuals who went to Carley Baptist Church as children, from the streets surrounding it, who have continued to attend a church somewhere all their lives"*, wrote one member. *"Sunday School and its teachers had the biggest impact on my life"*, wrote Pat, who has kept in touch with the church since moving away from the area: *"They opened up the Bible and gave me a love for the Lord. No praise is too high for them... They were truly angels to us, giving time and energy. They came in all weathers, through blackouts, from work, to take evening meetings. This will be echoed by lots of others... Some teachers still attend Carley, though not teaching, still proclaiming God's love"*.

Carley Street was the oldest but not the only Baptist chapel in the Wharf Street area. In 1872, around 90 members of the congregation of Trinity Baptist chapel in Alfred Street, Leicester, withdrew with their pastor Grey Hazelrigg, to form their own church. This was to become Zion Chapel, opened by the Society of Particular Strict Communion Baptists on a site between Humberstone Road and Erskine Street on 15 April 1873.

Though they were never so strong in numbers as the Baptists, the Wharf Street area also included a Congregational chapel in Willow Street, built around 1873 and closed in the 1930s, and number of Methodist chapels. The first was built in 1819 in George Street by the Primitive Methodists, and when it closed in the 1880s, it was purchased by the Ragged School Mission and incorporated into the Mission building. In Lower Hill Street, a Wesleyan chapel was opened in 1833 and demolished in 1930. As the population of the area continued to grow, another Primitive Methodist chapel was opened in Curzon Street in January 1860. It was was designed by Harry Shenton and one of Leicester's most distinguished architects, William Flint, who was also responsible for Charles Street Baptist Chapel, the Phoenix Assurance building in Welford Place (until recently used as a record library), and the lending library in Belvoir Street, built in the 1830s as a New Hall for the town's Liberals.

The building survived the redevelopment of the area in the 1960s, and was renamed All Saints in 1967 when its congregation joined with that of the Methodist chapel in Catherine Street. However, the mounting cost of repairs have made it difficult to maintain, and it is likely to be converted to another use in the future.

CANON HAROLD DRUMMOND

Many people have vivid memories of Canon Harold John Drummond, who was vicar of Christ Church for 42 years, and also priest-in-charge of the nearby St. Luke's church for some time. "As a child", recalls one man, "the towering personality was Canon Drummond - six foot six - who often walked through the area to his vicarage in Cobden Street. He wore a homburg or trilby hat, and touched it to everyone in greeting".

Rev. Drummond was ordained in 1906 and came to Leicester in 1914. He died in August 1982 at the age of 101. As his obituary in the Leicester Mercury noted, he was also "a lifelong fan of the Italian opera singer Caruso, and had written many articles about him, as well as helping to research several books".

CHRIST CHURCH AND ST. MATTHEW'S

The parish of Christ Church was formed from part of St. Margaret's parish in 1839 to cater for the expanding population of that part of Leicester, and covered most of the area to the west of Wharf Street between Humberstone and Belgrave Roads. The church itself was designed by William Parsons, architect of the prison on Welford Road, and of the County Lunatic Asylum - now the Fielding Johnson Building of Leicester University. Situated in Bow Street, it had 1200 sittings and cost around £6000.

The money was raised by subscription, and it was consecrated by the Bishop of Lincoln on 28 June 1839. An Elizabethan style parsonage was also built in Curzon Street in 1856. According to White's Directory in 1863, Christ Church was: *"built entirely of brick, in the Early English style... The centre window of the apse is filled with stained glass representing Our Blessed Lord... Above his head is depicted the Holy Spirit in the form of a dove, and at the bottom of the window is an angel bearing a scroll..."*.

However, with the new phase of building which followed the sale of the Wharf Street Cricket Ground in 1860, Christ Church proved too small to cater for an area now "densely populated", and in 1867 the parish was subdivided to form a second parish, that of St. Matthew. The church of St. Matthew was designed by the eminent architect George Gilbert Scott, and built by the Church Extension movement with the aid of *"large contributions of the nobility and gentry of the county, and of the manufacturers of the Borough"*. The foundation stone was laid by W. Percy Herrick on 4 October 1865 on the north side of Chester Street, *"of easy access to a vast number of street, occupied almost exclusively by artisans and the labouring poor in that rapidly increasing locality"*.

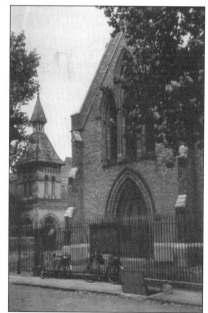

Its large number of free seats and its spacious interior, with broad aisles separated by tall slender pillars, earned it the name of the "Poor Man's Cathedral". *"There will be a free Gospel, a free church and ministry"*, reported the *Leicester Advertiser* on 7 October 1865:

"Nothing in the shape of payment will be required of them. Whatever of their substance, their benevolence and piety may prompt them to offer, will be used for the purpose of doing for others what is now being done for them - the building of free churches in districts where they are wanted... As this church is not erected in a fashionable locality... but for a hard working population, there can be no fear of its claim upon the consideration of the wise and benevolent being overlooked".

Christ Church in Bow Street
(Leicester Mercury)

The Early English style church was built of pink Mountsorrel granite with brick and Bath stone dressings, but was never completed - it was intended to have a tower and spire. This apart, however, wrote the *Advertiser* at its consecration in May 1867, nothing was spared

> *"to render it an elegant, as well as a commodious church. Not overdone with decoration, yet a pure taste has presided over the disposal of all parts of the building... what a halo of happiness, of ineffable delight, must have surrounded the hearts of all who had the remotest connection with the promotion of the honourable, the benevolent, the sacred undertaking".*

Between the wars, Christ Church was regarded as "low" church, and often held joint open air meetings with Carley Street Baptist church. However, the parish boundary ran along Wharf Street itself, and this caused some problems for residents on the west side of the street who preferred the "high" Anglicanism of St. Matthew's. *"I had to be married at a church I never went in. I never attended it in any way, shape or form"*, remembers Mrs Goss:

> *"and yet I could not be married at St. Matthew's, where I spent my childhood. And why? Because I was the wrong side of the street... the parish boundary...! It's all wrong... The vicar of Christ Church did say 'You don't attend this church, do you?', and I says 'No, I was always at Matthew's. I would have been married there'. 'But you're the wrong side of the street'. I says 'It don't matter what side you are, there's only one God...!'. But I had to get married at Christ Church...".*

Christ Church was closed in 1956 and the parish united with that of St. Matthew. It was demolished in the following year. However, St. Matthew's also fell victim to the general 20th century decline in churchgoing, as well as to the post-war redevelopment of the area; and after being closed for some years, it was eventually demolished in the 1980s. *"It's an awful pity that it was ever allowed to decay..."*, said Margaret Zientek:

"I remember a beautiful wooden statue of the Virgin, life-size, of the Virgin and child... We used to take the children to church on St. Matthew's Day, down to the mass - because it was an Anglo-Catholic church. And the whole school used to troop down there, the Junior school would come as well... and we'd have the mass in the church, and then afterwards the children would go home and have a half day's holiday... And we also took them to church on Ascension Day, and also for the Harvest, and the children used to bring their harvest gifts to school and there would be a long procession of children going down Taylor Street and round to the church... and the odd apple had a bite out of it by the time it got there!".

SALVATION ARMY

The Salvation Army was a familiar sight in the Wharf Street area. Originally based in Foundry Lane, on the opposite side of Belgrave Road, it also operated from Bread Street before its present citadel in Kildare Street was opened in 1935.

"Sunday nights in Gallowtree Gate, the Salvation Army used to play in the market" remembers Mr Britten, *"and then they used to march down Gallowtree Gate, down Humberstone Gate to the citadel in Kildare Street. And it would be lined - everybody would be there... watching the parade... Every Sunday night they'd have their sing-song in the Market Place...".*

Alderman Amos Sherriff JP, Mayor of Leicester in 1922 and a leading figure in the local Labour Party, was for many years an active member of the Salvation Army, *"parading the streets and preaching to the people what he felt to be the only cure for the greatest ill from which humanity suffered"*. The son of a glove knitter, he was born in Russell Street in 1856. He had virtually no schooling, but educated himself while working from the age of six and a half in a local brickyard. Later in life he became a cycle and china dealer.

In 1905 he was one of the organisers of the march of Leicester unemployed men to London, a major factor in the passage of new legislation to relieve unemployment later that year. He served as a Poor Law Guardian for 17 years, and in 1908 was elected to the Borough Council to represent West Humberstone, remaining on the Council with one short break until 1928, when he was elected an alderman.

CRAFTON STREET SYNAGOGUE

From the later 19th century, many Jews emigrated from Russia and Eastern Europe as a result of religious persecution and economic pressures. A small number of them came to Leicester itself, and like other immigrant groups, they tended to gravitate to areas of low-rent housing where other members of their communities were already living. It is no surprise, therefore, to find a Jewish Synagogue listed in street directories at 13 Crafton Street from around 1877 onwards, along with the names of its rabbis: N.J. Kowalski in its early years, followed by Rabbi Adolp Chodowski in the 1890s. As they became established in the town, the Crafton Street premises were replaced by a new purpose-built synagogue, designed by local architect Arthur Wakerley and opened in Highfield Street in 1898.

The Durham Ox pub in Birstall Street. The pub remains, but the surrounding area has been redeveloped (M & J Zientek)

WHARF STREET AT PLAY

Time and money are two of the main factors in determining what sort of leisure activities people enjoy. Women often had very little free time, particularly if they did paid work as well as looking after a house and family. In the 1920s and 30s, large numbers of the unemployed had plenty of time but little money. Those who did have work, however, were generally enjoying a rising standard of living, and could take greater advantage of commercial leisure facilities. The length of the average working week had also fallen since the turn of the century, although many people in Leicester still worked upwards of 50 hours a week.

PUBS AND CLUBS

Public houses were probably the main centre of leisure activities in any working class community. As a Mass Observation publication noted in 1943, *"the pub has more buildings, holds more people, takes more of their time and money, than church, cinema, dance-hall and political organisations put together"*. There were so many pubs in the Wharf Street area that it is impossible even to mention them all here. However, the drink itself was only one of their attractions.

In the words of one contributor to the St. Matthew's oral history, *"although people hadn't got any money they would always find a little bit to go into the pub and have a bit of company, and that was what it was all about..."*. They were a welcome escape from cramped and overcrowded homes - particularly for men, but for women too on Saturday nights and Sunday lunchtimes. *"My grandmother and a lot more ladies (went into pubs)..."*, recalls another: *"Sunday mornings you'd see them with the old cloth caps and they'd take the Sunday roast to be cooked while they went to the pub"*.

Young people were allowed into pubs when they were fourteen, *"but you couldn't drink. I did try it when I were 16, me friend and I went into a pub and we ordered a drink, a glass of beer each and then we got talking to these older men and talking about darts, the games they were playing, and one of them said 'Yes, these darts are older than what you two are', so we got up and ran out because we realised he knew we were under age"*.

Games like darts, dominoes and skittles were very popular, and regulars often came back for matches after they moved away from the area. Gambling was prohibited, as was music unless the pub had an entertainment licence - but by the 1930s several pubs had pianos, and singing was a regular feature of Friday and Saturday nights. All kinds of deals were done, goods bought and sold, and information exchanged about openings for jobs in the pubs. Several pubs in the area had originally catered for workers in particular trades - like the Braziers' Arms in Bedford Street, convenient for nearby foundries. Others, like the Oddfellows Arms in Gladstone Street, were meeting places for local branches of Friendly Societies.

Certain pubs had a reputation for being "rough", but few people could recall any serious incidents taking place inside them. Any "trouble" was largely confined to fights when

RAILWAY EMPLOYEES TOTAL ABSTINENCE SOCIETY

In the late 19th century, one of Leicester's lesser known temperance societies met at the Rutland Coffee House on the east corner of Wharf Street Humberstone Road. The Railway Employees Total Abstinence Society aimed to "promote the principles of total abstinence among the railway employees of the different companies in Leicester, and to assist the members during sickness or in case of accident". In 1888 it had over 100 members, and was still in existence in the early 20th century. The coffee house was one of several owned by the Leicester Coffee and Cocoa House Company, "the most formidable advocate of temperance existing. It combats temptation to imbibe intoxicants by providing nutritious, comforting and healthful beverages at the easy price of a penny a pint". It was opened in 1883 and demolished in November 1972.

they turned out on a Friday or Saturday night, but the police were hindered by the entries connecting the houses, which offered all sorts of escape routes. As Charlie Wright recalls, there were several pubs around Russell Square, and an island in the middle of the Square with a metal grit box, *"and you could stand on this on a Saturday night to see which one the fight would start from... there were women's lodging houses as well as men's round Britannia Street, and it was nothing to see the women stripped to the waist punching each other".*

"The ten o'clock turnout, if there wasn't a fight, we'd wonder what was up", recalled Mrs Goss as a child: *"too peaceful! And do you know what? It didn't just stop with the men fighting, the women would fight because they'd say 'Your husband's fighting my husband!' 'Well, he's a right to, he can do as he likes'. 'Oh no he can't!'. And they'd start. Down'd come the Black Maria...!".* In the 1930s, recalls Ernie Martin, *"there were a lot of ladies that used to be a little over the... they were drunk, there's no other word for it... they used to go along singing at ten o'clock at night because pubs had to come out at ten. There were lots of fights, but I don't suppose there was as much as there is today, to be honest".*

If there was less violence than today, it was also seen to be governed by unwritten rules on fighting "fair": fists and feet, and in the case of women, hair-pulling, scratching and tearing each other's clothes – but knives, bottles or similar weapons were rarely used. Other objects did fly on occasion, though, as the St. Matthew's oral history recalls. *"You'd get skirmishes at the weekend,*

The New Leicester Inn on Brunswick Street (M & J Zientek)

quite a lot of activity, you know, fights. I can remember one... where the windows got smashed in the pub... 'The Battle of Providence Place'... as far as I know it were two different families fighting about something or other and I think a chair or something went through the windows, not intentionally... I think somebody just picked up a chair and it went through the pub window".

During the war, there were also *"quite a few scuffles"* involving American servicemen stationed in the Leicester area. *"There were a lot of Americans round there... who all came flooding into the pub... the men resented it a bit, you know what I mean... everywhere you look you'd got the Americans with the girls and this, that and the other, and there was a bit of resentment, you know"*

LARRY GAINS AND THE JOLLY ANGLER

The Jolly Angler pub in Wharf Street had a gymnasium on its upper floor, where several well known boxers used to train. Among them were Reggie Meen, 'Pop' Newman and the Black boxer Larry Gains, who was born in Toronto, Canada, in 1900. His mother was the daughter of a former slave from Richmond, Virginia, who had escaped across the Canadian border, and his father's brother, Walter, was once amateur heavyweight champion of Canada.

Larry Gains himself began boxing in Canada, before pursuing his career in the USA and Europe. His first fight in Leicester was against Charlie Smith at Granby Halls in December 1930. In the following June he fought Phil Scott, the heavyweight champion of the British Empire, at Welford Road in front of a crowd of 34,000, knocking him out in the second round. According to a report in the Leicester Mercury on 15 June 1931:

'Gains was his master, temperamentally and as a boxer... Scott came in for a second with his left held straight out, and with the glove open. However, he made but a feeble attempt to lead with it... Gains swayed across, and hooked the right to the jaw, but he was not quite close enough, and Scott instinctively countered with a right to the ribs. This was his last blow, for Gains feinted, hooked the left to the jaw, followed similarly with the right, and then

The boxer Larry Gains, who trained at the Jolly Angler pub in Wharf Street, with his wife Ilse and children Harold and Otty (Courtesy of Harborough Museum, Leics. Museums, Arts & Records Service)

For some years the Great Mace of Leicester, the symbol of municipal authority, was displayed in the George III pub in Wharf Street. It was bought for £85 in 1836 by the landlady, Mrs Laughton - a staunch Tory - when the newly elected Liberal council auctioned off the civic plate. In due course it was sold for £135 to Col. Richard Ellison of Sandbrook Park, Lincoln. In 1866 the Borough Council itself bought it back for the original selling price.

flashed across the finishing punch - another right... At seven Scott was struggling, at nine he was on one knee and was feebly attempting to rise not "out". One or two people were obviously dissatisfied with the count, but the referee was indubitably right, for Scott was not in a position to defend himself at the 10th second...".

In all, Gains had 18 fights in Leicester between 1930 - 37 and won 17 of them. He was *"unusual to us because he was Black"*, Ernie White remembers:

"and you didn't see many Black men those days... Larry Gains was really a gentleman, he was one of the nicest fellows you could wish to meet... During this Jubilee (of George V in 1935)... he went the whole length of Wharf Street giving money away to the various street teas that were going on. He didn't make a big song and a dance about it, he just appeared in the street... he'd say 'Who's organising this?' ... and he went over and just slipped her a couple of pounds... This was the sort of thing he did without any sort of standing up and shouting".

In the 1930s, however, the Jolly Angler was also the scene of a contest for the "Heavyweight Championship of Wharf Street" between Charlie Till, a local butcher, and a florist named Jim Foulks. *"There was a wager went out... you know, amongst the green grocers and all, so that Butchy Hill, he put out a challenge to Jim Foulks... nobody else dared take him on, but Jim did...".* However, there are conflicting accounts of the result. In one, *"Jim went into the ring and he hit him once and he went out of the ring... he hit him once and he hit him clean out of the ropes"; and in the second, "it was declared a draw as neither landed a glove on the other".* Can anyone shed any light on this?

THE BOOT AND SHOE

The Boot and Shoe Working Men's Club in Wharf Street, otherwise known as the "Clog and Slipper", started life in the Trade Hall in St. James's Street around 1930. Charlie Wright - Member number 20! - recalls that the "bar" consisted of barrels placed on cloth-covered tables along one wall, and the "stage" of a rostrum with microphone in one corner. In its Wharf Street premises, the bar ran the whole length of the building apart from the entrance, with a second bar in the Concert Room on the first floor.

The Club did not cater solely for boot and shoe workers - affiliation to the Club and Institute Union (CIU) was dependent on it being open to the public at large - and most of its members lived locally. It soon became a meeting point for the community, one of the few places where families could enjoy a night out with their children, as well as adult company and practical help if needed from its welfare fund.

Regulars of the Oddfellows Arms in Gladstone Street soon after the end of World War II (Mrs P Pettitt)

The Boot and Shoe was also the first CIU club in Leicester to call bingo, an innovation inspired by a visit to a Nottingham club after a CIU cricket match. It was first tried at the weekly Wednesday evening dance, Charlie recalls, with the numbers pulled from a bag, and bottle tops or cardboard used to cover them on the bingo cards. Strict legal controls had to be observed, and the maximum that could be paid out in prize money in one session was £20 - but the crowds flocked in to play, and it proved a real "club saver" at a time when many Working Men's Clubs were struggling financially.

Live entertainment was provided on Saturday and Sunday nights, and Sunday lunchtimes - often by performers from the club circuit in the North, who would "do a turn" at two clubs over the weekend, dashing backwards and forwards between them. They included Ronnie Dukes and his wife, the comedian Hoggy Cooper, and the comedy duo Kitty and Billy Trevors. The Boot and Shoe was known as a "tough" audience, but local singers and comedians also had their chance to impress at the Tuesday "shop window", when budding club turns would perform for an assembly of CIU Club Secretaries. Gerry Dorsey - or Englebert Humperdink, as he later became - was among those who displayed their talents here, for no payment other than a pint of beer. For those who were engaged, the money compared favourably with other lines of work. *"I'd work Saturday night, Sunday dinner, Sunday night, for three pound ten shillings...",* recalled one former singer, and *"girls were working all week for that. I thought it was lovely money, just for a weekend. I was in my element".*

TWOPENNY RUSHES

One of the cheapest and most popular forms of entertainment for adults and children alike was the cinema. The Hippodrome was the main cinema for the Wharf Street area, but the Star on Belgrave Road was also popular.

The Hippodrome cinema at the corner of Wharf Street and Gladstone Street had a long and chequered history. Originally a three storey building, opened in 1862 as the Gladstone Hotel and Concert Hall, it seems not to have prospered, and in 1869 the *Leicester Advertiser* reported that the Hallelujah Band *"have engaged it for the purpose of holding religious services therein. Mr T. Greenbury, of Leeds, preached three sermons in the Hall on Sunday last"*. The Ragged School Mission took a seven year lease on the building in 1872, but by 1880 it had reverted to its earlier use under the title of the Gladstone Music Hall.

Three years later it was taken over by Sam Torr, landlord of the Green Man in Wharf Street, and opened as the Gaiety Palace of Varieties. *"The body of the hall contains a bar"*, it was reported, *"and for the accommodation of the audience numerous tables and chairs are provided..."*. The Gaiety was sold in 1885, and by 1895 it was known as the New Empire Theatre of Varieties. In November of the following year it featured one of the first cinematograph performances in Leicester, using a hand turned projector known as the "Animatoscope". The programme included such films as "Niagara Falls" and "The Emperor of Germany Reviewing His Troops", lasting around one minute twenty seconds. In 1900, patrons could also watch the "Bio-Tableau" showing scenes from the Boer War *"taken on the spot"*.

It became the Hippodrome cinema in 1922. In the meantime, a purpose built cinema - the Star - was opened on Belgrave Road in July 1914. *"Situated in the centre of a working-class district"* as the *Bioscope* described it, *"the new house has accommodation for 930 persons, and is replete with every convenience in the shape of up-to-date heating, ventilation and lighting..."*. Between the wars, the Star had a bit of a reputation as a "bug and flea pit". *"The Star had got a bad name..."*, Iris Smith recalls: *"We went to the Star this time, we'd heard they called it a flea pit, and we went to the box office and we said 'How much is it upstairs?', and she said 'There isn't an upstairs!'..."*. Unlike the Hippodrome, however, the Star promised an *"unimpeded view of the screen of generous proportions"*.

There was always a big crowd at the Hippodrome, remembers one woman who went there as a child, *"and the man stood there, 'Now take your time!'. Everybody made a rush to the box office, because... there used to be big pillars, and if you got last you got stuck behind the pillars, so you cricked your back and your neck or you didn't see at all..."*. In the 1930s, sixpence (2.5p) covered the cost of the cinema and an extra treat or two like sweets, a comic or a bag of chips. *"I used to go to the matinees Saturday afternoon"*, Iris Smith remembers: *"It was 2d, then it got that from the upstairs, which was 3d, that they'd throw things down on you, so I asked my mother if I could have the 3d to go upstairs..."*. In the 1920s, Harry Limbert recalls, adult patrons were said to have taken

The Hippodrome cinema on the corner of Wharf Street and Gladstone was originally a three storey building (Leicester City Council)

their supper to the Hippodrome with them, and *"it was commonly known as the 'Dripping Home', as it was mostly bread and dripping that they took"!*

The suspense of the weekly serials was one of the great attractions of the cinema. *"I used to go there (to the Hippodrome) quite a lot"* said Ernie Martin, *"because I did like Laurel and Hardy... We used to think that was fantastic, and Pearl White used to get strapped across the railway line... she'd be in trouble... somebody after her or something like that, and she'd..... the rope was hanging from the plane and, oh dear, she just missed it, or had she? 'See you next week'. It was always like that!"*.

Mrs Pettitt *"can always remember a little incident... I'd got to be a bridesmaid. Oh, I nearly went berserk... They bought me a frock, little hat and a basket of flowers, which they held then, you know, instead of a bouquet... I threw that across the room! Why weren't I going? I'd got to go! No! Pearl White was on, and she was on the railway line and I wasn't going to miss Pearl White! Never mind the wedding!"*. Mr Brown also has fond memories of watching *"cowboys like Hoppalong Cassidy, Buck Jones, Gene Autrey, the Masked Avenger, etc., or to see a serial, Flash Gordon... My favourite then, and I still wish I could see them again, was Tugboat Annie, starring Wallace Beery Senior, and Marie Dressler"*.

84

The Hippodrome closed in the 1940s, but two storeys of the building still remain and currently house a motor factor's business. The Star stayed open until 1958, and was in due course demolished to make way for a petrol station. Films were also shown at the Pavilion theatre - formerly the Prince of Wales and the Tivoli - on the corner of Belgrave Gate and Wilton Street. This was closed in November 1930, and the building demolished to make way for a road widening scheme.

At the Pavilion, said Ernie Martin, *"there used to be some very good turns on, and some very bad turns on too, and you knew when they were bad turns because they used to throw things... They'd throw paper or bags or rotten fruit. And they'd gracefully - on the stage, they'd gracefully move on!..."*. The theatre never matched the mass appeal of the "pictures", but by the Second World War the advent of radio was beginning to have some effect on cinema audiences. As Dorothy Rayson recalls, early radios consisted of crystal sets which had to be used with earphones, and *"the house would fill up with youngsters all eager to listen to the wondrous device known, appropriately as the Cat's Whisker... the crystal set. Later, my father and brother bought a do-it-yourself radio kit and built that from scratch, after which many happy hours were spent listening to the plays, news and music transmitted from it"*.

From the 1950s onwards cinema audiences were lured away in increasing numbers by television. This was well beyond the means of most families in Wharf Street in its early years, but as demand for sets increased, the price did eventually come down. Irene Holyoak recalls that *"our family was the first in the street (Metcalf Street) to have a television, for the Coronation in 1953. I couldn't get near it for all the family around it... It had a 12 inch screen, and we had it converted to Independent television while we were still living there"*.

A Fresh Air Fund outing in the 1930s from the Ragged School (Mrs D Rayson)

MEMORIES OF CHILDHOOD

Not surprisingly, given the lack of space at home, children spent much of their free time playing in the streets, or on the swings between Carley Street and Wheat Street. No one worried unduly about their safety. There was little traffic in the area in the evening, and *"there was never a time I daren't go out at night... nobody bothered us"*.

CHILDHOOD PASTIMES

Having said this, one woman does recall that the publican of the White Hart in Wharf Street threw buckets of water over children playing in the yard! Some children's games also fell foul of the prohibition against gambling in public places. Mr Brown remembers playing pitch and toss in the street, and *"we used to have a lookout to shout 'copper coming', when we all did a bunk"*.

Bill Pyne also recalls children being picked up by the police for playing shove halfpenny in the street, and taken to Woodboy Street Police Station for a ticking off. Scrumping, hitching a ride on a dray, and playing window tapping or "knock door run" were all likely to earn *"the odd clip"* from Sgt. George Hankinson. He lived at 20 Gladstone Street, but may be more widely remembered for playing the part of Daniel Lambert in the Leicester Pageant held at Abbey Park in June 1932.

One woman, who lived in the area during the First World War, remembers that *"we played hopscotch, skipping, tag, statues. We didn't really play with the boys. They had their own games - whip and top, marbles and so on. But it was safe to play out until dark because there was no traffic"*. There were plenty of activities which cost little or no money. Iris Smith remembers that ropes from orange boxes were used for skipping, and:

"we played snobs, double ball, hide and seek, hopscotch. We had a hoop and a stick that you'd roll down the street... all sorts of things like that, simple things. There was reading. We'd go to the library. It was amazing how busy we kept ourselves really. But I mean, that month's holiday from school used to seem endless... We used to collect fag cards as we called them, out the cigarette packets. Well, I hadn't got a father. He died when I was four, so we used to go on to Wharf Street when men left off work, and stop them and ask if they'd got any cigarette cards, and I mean, most of them were quite good. They'd give you them,

and we'd try to get a set... You used to play one another for cigarette cards, trying to get complete sets... And another thing we used to do was collect comics... we'd swap them... that was a regular thing. During the war especially we used to love it if we managed to get these American comics, which Flash Gordon was in, and Mandrake the Magician, but they were hard to come by, and I could never afford to have them bought me.".

One of the most popular games was "tin lurky". *"We had an old fruit tin or something, and we used to throw it, and you had to scramble, clear off quick, and then whoever it was had got to come round and find you"*. Once spotted, *"it was a race to see who could get back to the tin first"*. In the summer, however, if the weather was reasonable, children would spend much of their month's holiday from school on the local parks. *"Abbey Park we could walk up to, Spinney Hill Park we could walk to"*, remembers Iris Smith:

> *"but to get to Humberstone Park or Western Park, which was the favourite, we got a halfpenny return on the tram... but we had to be back on the tram for 5 o'clock, otherwise the halfpenny return was not valid... And when we used to get to the park, you see, we loved it because it was all the gullies up there, and we didn't know what to do with the tickets, so we'd put them in our shoes. Well, you could imagine, after we'd spent a few hours running and racing about, when we come to get the tickets out of our shoes, they were nearly disintegrated!".*

Those lucky enough to possess a bike might cycle up to Bradgate Park, always a popular spot. *"I remember my first bike"*, wrote Mr Brown, *"which cost £4 19s 6d (£4.98p), complete with pump and lights, from Curry's in the Haymarket. I learned to ride the hard way, coming down Kent Street hill on a full sized frame, fitted with pram wheels - no brakes - which we used to call our 'grid'. A well placed foot on the back wheel used to stop us near Humberstone Road. Some rides they were!".*

Ernie Martin and his friends *"used to go swimming at the Vestry Street baths, which was only across the road from Humberstone Road. That was for men only though, on a certain day, and ladies only on a certain day, and no mixed bathing, oh no! Mixed bathing came out later where the men had to wear extra... on the top, to cover all over, more or less"*. Boys also used to go swimming in the River Soar on hot days, Dorothy Rayson recalls, *"even though this was frowned upon - especially diving in from the Western Boulevard bridge in their underwear, and many's the time they were told off by the local policeman... "*.

Bonfire Night was one of the highlights of the year, recalls Mrs Pettitt, and *"they always had a great big bonfire at the bottom of the street - it's a wonder the houses never caught fire - they had a massive bonfire... We had fireworks. Used to hate 'em - still hate 'em, 'specially when they bang! - when they used to throw them... jumping jacks or something. Oh, I used to hate the lads then!"*. And talking of lads, said Mrs Goss, *"I wasn't allowed any boyfriends - seventeen, and I wasn't allowed to go out with any boys, so me and my pal... used to go to Aylestone boat house, and there was always a bridge in those days and we used to go and sit on the bridge. But you know, we were innocent, we never really thought about picking boys up, we liked to go where we could see the rowing boats...".*

FRESH AIR AND FUN

The Ragged School Mission in Bedford Street was responsible for arranging the local activities of "Pearson's Fresh Air Fund", a charity designed to give poor urban children a taste of the countryside. Each year a "treat field" was hired at Thurmaston, a short distance from the city, and each Saturday for three weeks 500 children and helpers would travel there by train from Leicester.

"Very few children today could realise the wonder and sense of adventure these ragged underfed children felt", writes Dorothy Rayson of the Fresh Air Fund trips:

> *"First the train ride into what - for them - was the unknown. Then disembarkation at Rothley, from where they marched crocodile fashion to the Treat Field, singing as they marched, the little ones being carried piggyback style. Once there, the wonders had only just begun. In the marquees were mounds of sandwiches and cakes, washed down with lemonade. For those who wanted it, games were organised. Cricket, football, sack races, egg-and-spoon and three-legged races. For others there was the delight of paddling in the stream at the bottom of the meadow, or climbing trees, or just daydreaming in the tall sweet-smelling grass... For those 1500 children, that single day in the country must have been a vision of near Heaven".*

"In the summer...", recalls Mrs Pettitt, *"they used to get a horse and cart, like a brake thing for them, they'd take them out in the country. I tell you where they used to bring them very often, to Penny's, you know, the Aylestone Lane, Wigston, that was where Penny's orchard and everything was... I roared my eyeballs up 'cos I couldn't go with them...".*

Sunday School outings from local churches and chapels were just as eagerly awaited. *"Races, prizes, lots of teachers used to join in the fun..."*, Pat Chapman remembers of the Carley Street chapel outings: *"Great excitement! Difficulty sleeping with anticipation... "*. Most Carley outings were also to nearby villages, but *"the most happy event"*, wrote Rev. Smith *"was our VE Day celebration when we took all the children on a Victory Outing to Skegness, which was the first time they had seen the seaside. People generously contributed to make this possible without charge"*. It was *"a headache for the teachers!"*, one remembers, but *"mercifully in all the excitement there were no casualties!"*.

"We used to get a star", remembers one contributor to the St. Matthew's oral history, *"and then we used to have an outing. I used to live for that day, we lived for it - because, you see, it was all cobblestones, we never seen a bit of grass"*. Ernie Martin went to St. Luke's Church on Humberstone Road: *"That's gone now, of course, and I do remember that they took us on an outing, a Sunday School outing in the summer, and the tramcars stopped outside the church... We all got on*

Skegness in the 1930s (Leicester City Council)

the tram, then up Humberstone Road and Humberstone Gate, across the Clock Tower, up High Street, round the juddering bend, over the river, over the canal, and it stopped there and we got off there, and we went on that railway that's now closed; been closed some time... West Bridge".

Paid holidays from work were a rarity in Leicester until the 1950s. Few Wharf Street families could look forward to a holiday by the sea, though they might manage a day trip to Skegness or other east coast resorts by train from the Great Northern station on Belgrave Road. Otherwise, the most they might expect was a stay with family or friends in the county, or a bus trip into the countryside.

"I used to stay with friends of my father in North Kilworth", remembers one woman as a child:. *"They had a thatched cottage, and I had my own room there - I had to share with my three sisters at home"*. Mr Britten was *"fortunate that some friends of the family were farmers... I used to go there for my holidays, because he used to come in every Saturday and bring chickens and eggs and all that sort of thing. I always went there for my holidays, except when we went to Skegness, which was about the furthest we went"*.

"The first holiday I had", Ernie Martin recalls, *"I think my father took me - he took me to Blackpool. I do remember the big wheel. Otherwise, I don't remember much... I joined the Scouts in Belgrave, and when I joined them I was asked if I would like to go on holiday, and we saved up our pennies... We went to Clovelly and had a wonderful time there... it was beautiful!"*.

Len Wilkinson, who attended the Ragged School Mission, recalled a camping holiday in Skegness in the late 1920s:

> *"Our means of transport to 'Skeggy' was on the back of a coal lorry kindly loaned by Ernest Lester, a coal merchant of George Street... Crammed onto the lorry with a marquee and all the other apparatus required for a week's camp was the highlight of the year for us. All this - and us - was headed, of course, by ex-RSM Bill Pyne, assisted by George Hawksley (who gave years of service to the Mission. George's employers, Fox Bros., potato merchants, used to donate sacks of spuds for the camp!).*

> *"One evening, when most of us were enjoying a night at Skeggy cinema, a terrific thunderstorm hit the town and flooded the cinema. Hurrying back to camp, we found the site devastated, with many families washed out of their small tents... Of course, the 'Man for All Seasons' was at the head of his troops, barking out orders for fires to be made... Piney's fieldcraft was second to none! He even managed to kindle fires from cow-pats!... At last we got our belongings into order, but Piney was not finished yet. 'Right lads', he said, 'let's give up our tent for the night for these mothers and children'. And so we marched to the Skeggy bowling green on the sea front, where we kipped down on deck chairs... A few lucky souls found refuge in the local police station!"*.

CHRISTMAS

For children who attended the Ragged School Mission, the annual Robin Breakfast on Christmas morning was one of the great highlights of the year. Even in 1890, as the Leicester Journal reported, the Christmas treat at the Mission was so popular that "no less than 300 tickets were distributed, but the youthful guests far exceeded that number and comprised not a few unassociated with the Ragged School".

The meal consisted of bread and butter, cake, meat patties and coffee, *"which the guests enjoyed to their hearts content"*. They then sang a Christmas Carol, *"not of course in the most correct time and tune, but with a hearty spontaneity befitting the occasion. Hardly had the carol ended when some mischievous sprite struck up 'Stop the Cab', and as if by magic 300 youngsters joined vociferously in the rollicking refrain of 'The Mystery of the Hansom Cab', to the evident perplexity of some of the fair waitresses"*. On leaving, each guest received a paper bag containing an orange and a mince pie, *"and it need hardly be added that they took their departure highly gratified with the entertainment"*.

Dorothy Rayson recalls that in the 1930s Christmas preparations began as early as October:

"With the festive season in mind, the Boys' Brigade and the Boy Scouts from other areas ventured forth into the wealthier areas of the city to collect toys and books no longer needed by their young owners. Many of these were broken, but that did not matter to children who had nothing. Boys and men set to mending them, whilst the girls and women sewed and knitted dolls' clothes and soft toys. That was not the end of the cornucopia. Mr Bonner was a commercial traveller dealing in expensive decorations for civil and other large occasions, and would arrive at the Mission with a huge hamper filled to the brim with Christmas goodies: beautiful crackers, cardboard plum puddings, snowmen and Father Christmases, all filled with small gifts. There was also bunting, tinsel, stars, glass robins and lovely shiny baubles to decorate the huge tree donated by someone else... I always managed to be around for the arrival of Mr Bonner and his marvellous hamper. I was too small to peep inside unless I stood on a stool, and once fell head first from my lofty perch into the basket, mortified at having shown my bloomers to all and sundry!...

"Food was donated too, mainly used as presents for older people - plum puddings, tinned goods, fruit and nuts, until the Mission was overflowing with goodwill from every part of Leicester. By the time Christmas came, every child had been presented with a present, and every pensioner with a box of food. In addition to this were the parties! Rows of trestle tables in the big hall, groaning with sandwiches, jellies, cakes, lemonade, tea, and of course, Mr Bonner's wonderful crackers!".

A Robin Breakfast on Christmas morning in the 1890s (Mr W Pyne)

There were no lavish presents even for children from better off families, however. In the St. Matthew's oral history, Mrs Elsie Wood (nee Johnson) recalls that on Boxing Day *"we used to go down the shops, up to a certain time of day if you spent a ha'penny there she would give you an orange. Of course your aunties would give you some coppers, didn't buy you presents in them days. You used to hang your stocking up and you'd perhaps get snakes and ladders, an apple and a few nuts".*

Even so, said Ernie Martin, Christmas was *"marvellous... decorations inside... balloons and so on and cards. Used to go out singing and get pennies. You see, as kids, we didn't feel the cold till we got in home, and then, know what I mean! Outside and your face is all aglow... we enjoyed ourselves"*. At Christmas, someone else recalls, Wharf Street itself *"looked like fairyland. The shops were dressed up with paper chains, and lit by gaslight or paraffin lamps"*.

MEMORIES OF THE R101 AIRSHIP

Many people have vivid memories of the R101 flying over Leicester in 1929, "like a giant cigar flying majestically through the sky".

The 777 foot long airship appeared unexpectedly during a flight from its base at Cardington in Bedfordshire, and *"I remember gazing up in awe... "*, wrote Mr Brown: *"it was just after one o'clock, and I got a good hiding for saying 'Ain't it bloody big'...!"*. According to a report in the *Leicester Mail* on 18 October 1929, the airship:

"passed over Leicester shortly after 1 pm today...The arrival of the R101 took Leicester by surprise. Coming from an easterly direction, she could not be sighted from any of the highlands in the city, and at 1.25 pm she was right over the Humberstone end before watchers were aware of her presence. The first impression was of a huge shadowy bulk moving slowly but irresistibly across the grey cloud background. Heading against the wind she made no noise, and the sight of the huge monster forging silently ahead was curiously uncanny... When she was almost directly over the Town Hall Square, she slowed down her engines, dipped her nose in salutation to the city and the thousands of upturned faces of her citizens, then shot ahead at full speed to demonstrate her power...".

The R101 crashed near Beauvais in France on 5 October 1930, on its way to India. *"Rain and a faulty engine forced it to fly low over the Channel"*, according to one report, *"and to keep low when it reached France. By that time the airship was seen to be pitching and rolling. Shortly before 2 am... the R101 suddenly dived. In a desperate attempt to gain height, water ballast was pumped from the airship, but it sank to the ground and burst into flames"*. One witness said *"it looked as if the whole world had exploded"*.

There were only six survivors, and *"Leicester has more than one reason for personal grief at the loss of the R101 and the terrible death roll involved... Both Sir Sefton Branker and Lord Thomson were members of the Leicestershire Aero Club. Sir Sefton flew to Leicester only three weeks ago with Miss Amy Johnson"*. Also killed in the disaster was Sidney Ernest Scott, one of the crew, who lived in Milligan Road in Leicester.

SCHOOL

NO ENTRY

St Matthew's Infants' School in Brunswick Street (Mrs M Zientek)

S C H O O L D A Y S

Until the 1870s, the great majority of schools in England were run by charitable or religious organisations, and the Wharf Street area was no exception. By 1846, the Leicester Infant School Society had opened a school in Metcalf Street. Christ Church school was opened in Bow Street in 1840 with space for 350 pupils, and a second school, *"a handsome brick building"* capable of accommodating 480 boys, girls and infants followed in 1852 in Curzon Street. This was transferred to St. Matthew's church when Christ Church parish was divided. Two more schools attached to St. Matthew's were opened in Brunswick Street and Chester Street in 1869, along with a Wesleyan school in Clyde Street two years earlier. All three were no doubt built with planned reforms to the education system in mind - by ensuring that there were already ample school places in the area, they would not have to compete with publicly funded schools provided by local authorities under the 1870 Education Act.

LOCAL BOARD SCHOOLS

The oldest schools in the area seem to be the British Schools in Hill Street, opened in 1831. The schools were run by the Nonconformist British and Foreign Bible Society - hence their title - and had around 650 pupils of both sexes in 1846. In that year, the school was still using older children - "monitors" - to teach younger ones, although this system was falling out of favour.

According to the Inspector's Report, the boys' school *"under a practised master of industry, energy and invention, is a good study of what can be accomplished on the monitorial plan by one teacher in the instruction of 300 children... each monitor has his appropriate manuscript manual of arithmetic and geography, and his school-made map, to help him in these departments... and the discipline of the whole is perfect...".*

The schools were closed in 1893, but funds from the sale of the premises were used to set up the Hill Street British School Exhibition Fund, providing scholarships for evening pupils to study at the Leicester School of Art. However, despite the efforts of other churches and chapels, in 1867 the

Leicester Unitarian Domestic Missionary Joseph Dare calculated that only half of the estimated 14,000 children in the town between the ages of 6 and 14 were receiving an education. After 1871, the Leicester School Board began to build new schools to remedy the shortage of places. The first of these, a large brick building with accommodation for almost 1000 children, was opened in Syston Street on 19 January 1874 at a cost of £6620.

Its first headmaster, Lawrence Staines, was at one time president of the North Midland Union of Elementary Teachers, a body instrumental in securing an annual summer holiday for teachers - two weeks, taken in rotation, so that school fees were not lost. A second Board School was opened in 1877 in Christow Street, to replace the old Infant School Society school in Metcalf Street. This met with much opposition from the local church schools, on the grounds that they would be *"exposed to undue competition"*. Having conducted a survey of the area, however, the School Board concluded that there were far more children between the ages of three and thirteen in the area than there were school places, *"so that when the new school in Christow Street is built to accommodate 450 children, there will still be a deficiency of 984 places"*.

The two-storey school cost just under £5500. It was *"evidently built as if it is meant to last and be useful for some time to come"*, the *Leicester Advertiser* reported: *"The site itself is perfect for a school. Standing in the middle of a thickly populated district, it nevertheless occupies an open space formed by the juncture of three streets - Lewin-street and Providence-street, with Christow-street on the eastward front. The school will no doubt prove a valuable addition to the educational machinery of the town"*.

It was at Christow Street school that Leicester's first Nursery class opened in March 1929. *"About 30 children can be admitted to this school at the age of three..."*, the *Leicester Evening Mail* reported:

> *"They begin the day by playing with their wonderful variety of toys and games, and meanwhile, one by one they are washed and their teeth cleaned... there are a great many exciting things for everyone to do, including looking at picture books, and learning to differentiate colours, by means of little discs, similar patterns, similar shapes. The whole of the activities of the day are directed towards preparing the children for their next year at school and the year after that... the whole school has an air of happiness, or freedom and ease, miles removed from the stiff discipline of the old style school"*.

Further Board Schools followed, the last of them in Willow Street in 1884. A short-lived venture in Gladstone Street, opened in 1880 to take over the work of the Ragged School Mission's day schools, was itself replaced by the Milton Street Board School in 1883. The school was *"situated in one of the most thickly populated parts of the Borough..."*, noted the *Leicester Daily Post*:

> *"the handsome building stands out in bold relief amid the lesser structures by which it is surrounded... Mr J. Ellis, in proposing a vote of thanks to the Mayor, remarked that as*

civilisation advanced wealth seemed to increase among certain classes of the people; but at the same time poverty seemed to increase in their large towns. Education seemed to be the only means of enabling them to help their fellow men, to put them in a position to claim what was their right, and what was payment for what they did for others...".

In 1892 a special class for children with learning difficulties - "defective" in the language of the time - was opened at Milton Street. Lessons were limited to a maximum of 15 minutes, and *"the education of the hand and the eye was made an instrument to lead up to a small amount of book learning"*. Such classes were almost unknown outside London. After 1885, the school also housed an evening school for men and youths, paying a fee of one penny for each class.

Willowmead Girls' School in 1962, originally Willow Street Board School (Leicester Mercury)

ATTENDANCE VERY LOW...

Church and chapel schools were not replaced by the Board schools, but continued alongside them. In 1874, St. Luke's church on Humberstone Road opened new schools for 540 children in Gladstone Street , but all schools faced similar difficulties. First and foremost was that of getting the children to attend them. This was a constant worry, because until the 1890s, under the system of "payment by results", government grants to schools were in part dependent on the number of children in regular attendance.

Unless it was essential for particular types of work, many people placed little value on education in the later 19th century; but even if they did, some families - particularly those with several children - could not afford to pay the fees. At the Board schools in the 1870s these were 2d (1p) a week, but added to this was the loss of the children's earnings while they were at school.

In a typical entry, the Log Book of St. Matthew's School in Chester Street in July 1870 noted *"a large number of the children absent during the last week or two, either at work or because their parents are unable to pay the school fees"*. Illness was another common cause of absence. *"Numbers rather low due to the prevalence of smallpox"*, St. Matthew's Curzon Street School reported in March 1872; and at Christow Street school in June 1900, *"the attendance throughout the week has been exceptionally poor owing chiefly to illness. There are four cases of diphtheria reported, two of which have been fatal"*.

Until quite late in the 19th century, most workers in Leicester were not tied to the discipline of factory hours. To a large extent, they could set their own hours of work and take their leisure when it suited them - and these habits were passed on to their children. *"Have great difficulty in getting the children here in time"*, it was noted at Christow Street in February 1879: *"The parents seem to have the idea that their children might be allowed to come in school at whatever time they may think proper to send them"*. At Chester Street in July 1870, *"A very poor school... Most of the children absent to see a circus"*; and two days later, *"very few children present due to a flower show being held at Belgrave"*. The Cavalry review, the annual fair and the Races were also cited at various times as causing mass absenteeism.

Attendance did tend to improve as more parents became accustomed to the discipline of factory work, and as rising average incomes made fees less of a problem. However, fluctuating numbers did mean that classes were smaller than they would have been with full attendance. In 1872 Curzon Street had 350 pupils on roll, taught by the headmistress and six pupil teachers older girls with no formal training. Nor surprisingly, they often had difficulty maintaining discipline. Several were reprimanded for striking children, and at Chester Street in 1878, one pupil teacher was dismissed on the grounds that *"she has no energy and not the slightest idea of keeping her class in order, let alone teach the children"*. In the following year, one was *"cautioned... against reading books during the time she ought to devote to the instruction of the children in the classroom"*.

Reading, writing and arithmetic took up much of the curriculum, but the children were also taught History and Geography, and - at Christow Street for a time in the late 1870s - French. To equip them for their expected roles as wives and mothers, the girls learnt needlework, "domestic economy" and laundry work, attending classes in the latter at Charnwood Street School. The boys were encouraged to take up sport, which was seen as character forming as well as encouraging better health. *"I have started a cricket club for the boys..."*, it was noted in the Chester Street Log Book in 1912: *"A match was played with Harrison Road school, who won easily. The boys were downhearted, but I spoke to them regarding success coming out of failure (even in life) - if the reason for failure is noted"*.

Empire Day on 24 May was marked each year by special activities. At St. Matthew's school in Curzon Street in 1905, *"a short lesson will be given this morning by each teacher on our 'Empire' - its size; people; and how these various parts have been acquired. This lesson will be given instead of the usual domestic economy lesson... at 11. 30 am the children will assemble in the main room to sing the National Anthem; to salute the flag; and the Higher*

Taylor Street School (Leicester City Council)

Juniors will give a short address appropriate for the occasion...". In the earlier 20th century, there were also occasional educational outings. In 1908, for instance, children from Curzon Street were taken to Wombwell and Bostock's Menagerie on one of its regular visits to Leicester. The visit, which was *"thoroughly enjoyed, should prove of educational advantage to the children, as the exhibits include some rare specimens of animals".*

MEMORIES OF SCHOOL

Several of the schools in the Wharf Street area had closed by the early 1930s. They included the Hill Street British schools, St. Luke's in Gladstone Street, and Clyde Street Wesleyan school, which was transferred to the control of the Local Education Authority (LEA) in 1924 and closed four years later. Financial difficulties and inadequate premises played a part, but the declining population of the area was the main factor. This fell by about 3000 between 1921-31, and the movement out of the area was speeded up by the clearance programme of the 1930s.

"In spite of the recent extension of the area on which the school draws", noted an Inspector's report of Christow Street school in 1938, *"the numbers have steadily declined during the past four year. Demolition of slum property in the neighbourhood and the continued transfer of families to other parts of the city account mainly for this fall in numbers".* Christ Church school was taken over by the LEA in 1925, but St. Matthew's Curzon Street school closed in 1936, and Milton Street in 1938, with pupils being dispersed to other local schools.

Milton Street became a Feeding Centre during the war, and was then used as a central school kitchen before becoming an Education Department store. Others, like Willow Street, had become intermediate schools, catering for children from the age of 11 or 12 until they left school at 14. However, a new school was opened in Taylor Street in 1932, when it was still planned to improve rather than demolish parts of the area. *"Even I can't remember the iron frame being erected",* wrote Mr Brown, *"but it stood as a rusty hulk before building started. At first, we thought it was going to be a factory, until it was announced in the press as being a new school. As far as I know, it was the only school in Leicester with four playgrounds, one each end, one on top, and one in the basement, which was used in wet weather".* Taylor Street compared favourably with older schools in the area. Dorothy Rayson started at Christ Church school when she was five, and remembers it as:

"truly Dickensian... The schoolroom was long and narrow and very cold in winter, for the only heating was a little black stove filled with coal. The room was filled with narrow desks and wooden forms with no backrests. The class had about 60 children of all ages. Teacher sat on a high-backed chair on stage, so she could see all the children, and the blackboard - the main instrument of tuition - hung on the wall. What few books we had were really dilapidated... The inkwells were filled with black sludge, and the pen nibs were always crossed, but it was only when blots bespattered a page that a new nib was reluctantly presented".

Nursery class at St. Matthew's Infants' School in the 1940s, playing in the yard. (Mrs M. Zientek).

She later went to St. Matthew's school in Chester Street, where *"I was very happy... but it was still the same old story. The school was as deprived as the area it was in. All the books were out of date, and there was no library..."*. Ernie Martin, who lived in Eldon Street at the top end of Wharf Street, went to Clyde Street Wesleyan school, and then to Willow Street Intermediate School, popularly known as "Willy's":

> *"You had to move when you were about 11, and we had to go down to Willow Street, which was a very, very long way in those days to me. It was right down beyond Russell Square... We used to have a teacher called Mr Vann, who played the violin, and he used to teach us, in serial form, 'Treasure Island' by Robert Louis Stevenson... Miss Francis, she used to teach us in the morning, religion... and she used to serialise Creation, and the beginning, and the crossing of all the Egyptians. I can see it now - 'And the Egyptians are on one side, and we wanted to cross onto the other... and the seas all came up. I'll tell you all about it next week!'. Used to always finish that way...".*

Discipline was generally strict, and little time was spent investigating who was at fault. In the 1930s, said one woman, *"I remember the teacher we had at Taylor Street... she was a good teacher really... until the day some of us were caught talking, and I was ever such a quiet little child and I'd said just two words at that time, and she got the whole lot of us and out came the black cane and we got it good and proper! I went home with a stinging palm. I wouldn't mind, but I'd only said two words, you know..."*.

At Milton Street around the time of World War I, another woman remembers, lessons consisted mainly of the three Rs: *"no nonsense, no fancy subjects"*, and one of the teachers was *"very handy with the cane - you got a thump on the fingers if you got the answer wrong. The boys were always being caned on the hand for something"*. However, it was the cinema rather than the cane which motivated one woman who attended the same school in the 1920s: *"I went to Milton Street till I was 12. Now, we had to learn, because if we didn't learn, and we went to the pictures, we'd got to be able to read to know what the writing said - there was no talking on the films!"*.

School inspectors, and perhaps some teachers themselves, seem to have had low expectations of the pupils. According to His Majesty's Inspector (HMI) in March 1924, the children of Christow Street school *"come almost exclusively from poor homes and depend on their teachers far more than is usual for much that is outside the ordinary school syllabus... A high standard of attainment in the fundamental subjects is not to be expected; what is necessary is a firm foundation of real though elementary knowledge, conveyed to the children in as concrete a form as possible"*.

However, as further report in 1938 suggests, schools were also seen as playing an important role in "socialising" the children of the area. *"The school continues to do valuable work in what is still one of the poorest quarters of the city..."*, said the HMI report in that year, it *"should not, however, be judged on academic results alone. It plays an important part in the social structure of a neighbourhood of this description. The formation of correct habits of speech, behaviour, cleanliness and consideration for others become largely the task of the teacher"*.

None of the local schools had a playing field, and the children had to travel elsewhere for sports. At Chester Street school, Dorothy Rayson remembers: *"sporting activities were organised for a half day every week. For this we had to go by tram to the gasworks on Aylestone Road, where there was a sports field and club house."*

Pat Chapman remembers that at Taylor Street in the later 1940s, *"we had a good netball team, playing against other schools. The teachers took us after school on public transport. We also went swimming at Cossington Street baths - if you owned a bathing costume - but only in the Fourth Year... It was a very happy time. I loved it"*. As children, many people from the Wharf Street area also attended the Open Air School at Stocking Farm. *"The school was situated in an open field where sheep grazed and a pond supported frogspawn and dragonflies..."*, Dorothy recalls, and *"at break time the children dashed off to the pond, and the stream at the bottom of the field, where they splashed about happily until the time of the next lesson. Not that much work was ever accomplished! Going there was intended to improve health, not education!"*.

However, some people have less happy memories of their schooldays. *"I must admit I didn't like school. I mean, really... I couldn't wait to leave to get to work..."*, said one woman. After the war, said Irene Holyoak:

> *"I started at Christow Street Infants, and I hated it. I came home more times than I stayed, and eventually I didn't go to school again until I had to when I was five. I remember having to have cod liver oil when I was at Christow Street, and I hated that as well. Then I went to Taylor Street. I had trouble learning to read and write, but the teachers encouraged me and I passed the Eleven Plus. I went to the Gateway, but I wasn't keen on it...".*

She was still more fortunate than many who passed the Eleven Plus exam, and were offered a place at a grammar school - only to realise that the family's finances could not bear the additional costs involved. *"The pity of it was, I passed the Eleven Plus exam, you know"*, said Mrs Pettitt: *"and I could have gone to Wyggeston Girls' school, but we were so poor, they couldn't afford to buy my clothes... there were no social services in them days that bought you clothes and your books and all that sort of thing. So they had to go up to - I don't know where it was, Magistrates' Court or something... to explain the circumstances, to tell them that I couldn't possibly go because they hadn't got the money to send me. I often wondered about it...".*

ST. MATTHEW'S INFANTS' SCHOOL

Margaret Zientek (nee Barrass) has contributed these memories of St. Matthew's Infants' School in Brunswick Street. She taught the Nursery class there throughout the Second World War.

Lucy Diamond was 25 years Head of the Infants' school. People used to call her the Governess... Louise Flavell was there at least within a year or two of Lucy going... so they worked together for many years. She did a tremendous amount of social work - she was one of the pioneers of nursery education... she got milk for these children, they'd pay a little bit for it, they would collect clothes...

There was one big hall, two small classrooms behind it, very tall... they went up into these great rafters, each room did, but they were quite narrow, so that at one end there were three classes of 60 in that one hall divided by screens... The toilets were in the yard - they were trough toilets, and the boys had a stand-up piece which we used. As we only had a part-time caretaker, I used to take a bucket of disinfectant out every now and again and would chuck it up the wall, because they used to have competitions, you know, like little boys do! There were two little brown cold water sinks in the cloakroom and one stone sink, and that must have been the washing facilities for 440 children at one time. And it was still about 150 when I went there... There was no central heating whatsoever. There were huge "tortoise" stoves filled by coke and a range round them that would sometimes get red hot, and you put the milk bottles round in the winter to thaw the milk out...

At the time I went there, there were five classes, so five teachers and the Head... Lucy used to have a Christmas party to which she would invite all the old staff... so I got to know the staff of long before. Mrs Dickenson had been there many, many years before when it was a baby room, and she would tell me how the babies (3 year olds) were actually penned in. There were little seats around the wall on which the baby sat, and then you pulled a tray over their heads and there they were, penned in...

I had 30 children and I had no helpers. You managed them - hard work, but you managed them. You had to put them to bed in the afternoon in little folding beds, and you had to change the sheets on a Friday... All the children wore nursery overalls which all had to go home every week to be washed - and you did all your own secretarial work because there weren't any secretaries.

Mrs Dickenson remembers - there were no school dinners of course in those days... they used to cook their own dinners, and she remembers sitting shelling peas once when this Inspector came in, she was shelling this bowl of peas under the table trying to hide it under her skirt!

In the Nursery it was stories, music and a sleep in the afternoon, poetry, little scripture stories, you would tell them... bits of painting and drawing... we had puzzles, and dollies and things - a lot of it was home-made by staff - dressing up things, and the old wind-up gramophone I used to take with the 78 records... They started reading seriously at five.

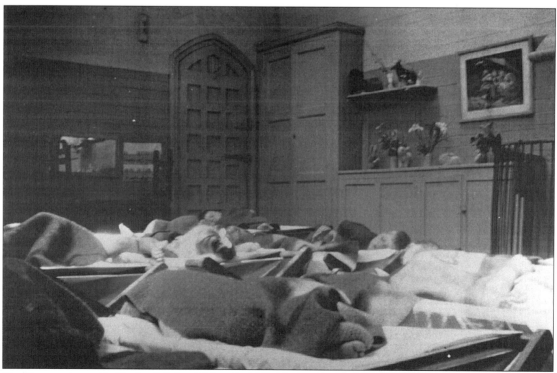

The Nursery class at St. Matthew's Infants' School in 1941 (M. Zientek)

Damage to the Freeman Hardy and Willis factory in Rutland Street, following the "Leicester Blitz" on 19 November 1940 (Leicester City Council)

WHARF STREET AT WAR

Wharf Street shared the experience of other areas during the Second World War. Local men and women were conscripted into the armed forces or directed into civilian occupations. Factories were turned over to the production of munitions and other essential items, and women replaced men on the factory floor, receiving the full male rate of pay for the job on the strict understanding that the man would reclaim it once hostilities ended. *"Everyone of a certain age had to register for some kind of war work"*, writes Dorothy Rayson: *"My friend Jessie and I were sent to work in the goods yard at the Great Central Railway. This was heavy work, with long hard hours. We had to get up at 3.30 am to be at work by 4.15 am, leaving off in the middle of the afternoon completely exhausted after carting tons of material from one wagon to another"*.

THE DAY WAR BROKE OUT

People learnt to live with shortages and rationing, with the blackout, the constant fear of air raids and the anxiety for loved ones serving overseas. Evacuees came and went, and in the later stages of the war, US servicemen and Italian and German prisoners of war added to the city's population. At the beginning of the war, however, few had any idea of how long the conflict would last, or of the far-reaching effects it would have on their lives. *"I remember the Sunday that war broke out"*, said Ernie White:

> *"and we were all waiting to hear Neville Chamberlain on the radio at 11 o'clock, because as you appreciate, you got your news then either by radio or by special newspapers... and it was just about a second to 11 o'clock and this old dear came in... and she said 'Two pen'orth of snuff, Ern'. I said, 'Well, you'll have to hang on a moment, darling, Mr Chamberlain's going to tell us whether we're at war or not'. 'Oh, don't worry about that, I want my snuff!'... Anyway, I sort of kept her hanging about till Chamberlain gave his speech... and I said... 'Well, that's it, darling! We've got the gloves off now...'. So I*

gave her the snuff, and she tipped it out on the back of her hand... she had a good sniff of her snuff, and five minutes later she was back again for another two pen'orth. The penny had dropped, it had hit her. She'd suddenly realised that the way of life that we'd known for many years was in danger of falling away...".

Around 30,000 people were evacuated to Leicestershire in the first few days of the war alone, but many soon drifted back home. *"The Mission had two evacuees for a short time"*, Dorothy Rayson remembers, *"two boys from the East End of London. One was too young to be called up, and the other had a withered arm. They were both 'terrors', and we had an awful job with them! Billeted in the Mission itself were two complete families, in rooms hastily furnished for them. None of the evacuees stayed long. Leicester held no attraction for them, and in spite of the heavy bombing in London, they all returned there".*

It was an anxious time for children whose fathers were called up, as one contributor to the St. Matthew's oral history remembered: *"Me Dad had joined up and he was called the week before war broke out. I was at home, and all I can remember is the speech coming over that war had been declared with Germany, and I started bawling because I thought me Dad was going to be killed, but he never moved out of England. He never went further than Northampton, and he got booted out because I sent him a birthday card with forty nine kisses in the shape of 49 and he was too old, he forged his age to get in, and they discharged him and he joined the Home Guard'...".*

"DID BABY JESUS HAVE SWEET COUPONS?"

Leicester had no large concentrations of wartime industries, and it was not a major target of bombing raids. Even so, it did not escape altogether, and suffered heavy casualties during a prolonged attack on 19 -20 November 1940. The Freeman Hardy and Willis factory on the corner of Rutland Street and Humberstone Road was one of several properties severely damaged during the raid.

Many local people still have vivid memories of that night. *"We lived in Eaton Street, which is about halfway down"*, recalls Mrs Beryl Doughty, who was then in her teens:

"and at that particular time no siren had gone off or anything like that. We were at the (Ragged) School Mission... we were rehearsing and things for Christmas pantomimes, shows and that sort of thing... and my father came dashing in to say we had to get out because they were dropping bombs... It was the first thing we knew about it, and we had to run along Wharf Street... Well, we got into the Anderson shelter in the garden... but by then Freeman Hardy and Willis was well on fire, and we got all the burnt rubbish and all that, blowing, see, and it was all coming down... The next morning, to see all the damage... You couldn't quite believe it had happened in the night".

The next morning, said Margaret Zientek:

"we went to school, and there were 13 children in the school because they'd all been in the shelters all night long. They were right in the centre of the city. There wasn't a pane of glass touched in the school, but... it had hit the undertaker's (George Stanion) on the other side of the road... At lunchtime I went down to the end of Brunswick Street, onto the Humberstone Road, and I went as far as Freeman Hardy and Willis's factory, which was just a smouldering shell".

Rationing of food and other items was introduced very early in the war, while other items which were not actually rationed were often in short supply. As a child, remembers one woman: *"We used to queue up at the Maypole, you know, the grocers. Me and me brothers used to pretend we didn't know each other, so we could get a few extra bits and pieces. If you saw a queue, you'd go and join it. We didn't know what we were queuing for until we got to the front!"*. Imported fresh fruit was very difficult to come by. Margaret Zientek recalls a child bringing an orange to school one day, *"taking it all round the school. Her father, who'd come from abroad, had brought an orange... later they had the odd banana, and they didn't even know what to do with them, they'd never seen one"*.

Children were most directly affected by sweet rationing. *"I remember my mother cut out all the little sweet coupons very carefully from the ration book once"*, said one woman, *"and put them somewhere and promptly lost them. And about six months later we found them and couldn't get the sweets because they were out of date!"*. Many children had never known sweets to be freely available, and regarded rationing as a fact of normal life. *"I'd got my class sitting in front of me once"*, Margaret Zientek recalls, *"and one little boy piped up: "Teacher, did Baby Jesus have sweet coupons?'..."*.

For local shopkeepers, rationing brought problems of a different kind. *"I remember the job of counting coupons every week"*, said one, *"which was a hell of a boring job... you know, some for food, some for cheese, some for sweets, piles and*

Ernie White home on leave in 1940, outside the family's Brook Street shop. (Mr E White)

Retirement of Miss Lucy Diamond, Headmistress of St. Matthew's Infants' School in 1941. Miss Diamond is in the centre, and Miss Louise Flavell, who succeeded her as head, on her right. (Mrs M Zeintek)

piles that had to get sent off". Mrs Goss, who kept a grocer's shop in Wharf Street during the war, remembers that *"you were not supposed to sell anything without a coupon, but me, oh I did. Coventry was being bombed, a lady came in and she said 'I haven't got any coupons'. I said 'Don't worry about it, love'... so she said 'Well, I want some tea and some sugar and bananas, and so and so'. So she paid, and she says 'I'll have you now', she says. She was an inspector..."*.

To supplement their own rations, people could buy meals at subsidised restaurants in the area. During the war, an open space where Lee Circle car park now stands served as a parking place for military vehicles. Also on the site was a British Restaurant, housed in a long low building, and providing low cost meals for workers from local factories and businesses. Another larger British Restaurant, open day and night to cater for shift workers, air raid wardens and others on call, operated in Colton Street, on the opposite side of Humberstone Road. The Lee Street restaurant remained open for some years after the war, and was listed in a local directory in 1951 as the Central Civic Restaurants.

WARTIME MEMORIES OF CARLEY STREET BAPTIST CHURCH

During the war, the congregations of local churches and chapels were swelled by evacuees, servicemen and women, and - in its later stages - prisoners of war. "Being a teenager during the war years", remembers one member of Carley Street Church, "I saw English and American servicemen mingled with the congregation... then German prisoners of war when they were allowed out of their camps on the outskirts of the city".

Rev. P.J. Smith became Pastor of Carley Street in 1941, and also ministered to members of the US 82nd Airborne Division who were stationed in the county in 1944. *"When the USA became our Allies"*, he recalls,

> *"we also gained some American friends and helpers, including Chaplain Henry Wall. I was privileged to substitute for him for 12 weeks when he went with his men on the D-Day invasion. As far as I know, I was the only British Pastor to have that privilege. A jeep came to take me to the camp to conduct the Protestant service, then rushed me back to Carley Street where one deacon had started the morning service, and I was always in time to preach the sermon!...*

> *"During the war, practically every Sunday after the Church Service, we conducted Open-air Meetings in Humberstone Gate near the Hot Dog Stall. We normally gained a good attentive audience, though sometimes we were pelted with bits of the hot dogs!".*

As many people will remember, the hot dog stall was on the site of the ornamental horse trough which used to stand in Humberstone Gate, at the top end of Wharf Street. Rev. Smith also recalls that:

> *"One winter we hired the Free Thinkers' Hall (Secular Hall) to get crowds of young people in off the streets to hear the Gospel. One year we closed the Church for three Sundays when we had a large blacked-out marquee for hearing a well-known Irish Evangelist, Peter Connelly... That marquee was erected on the land where the present Church now stands...*

> *"During the war, a group of Christian businessmen were able to rent property on London Road to turn the upstairs into an attractive Forces Institute run by volunteer workers. I was chairman of that Committee. I always finished my busy Sunday after our Open-air Meeting in Humberstone Gate by going to meet the men and women of the forces gathered there. The late Frank Osborne and Alfred Finnie were leaders of this successful provision for the pleasure of forces personnel."*

Brunswick Street before redevelopment (M & J Zientek)

THE FACE OF LEICESTER IS CHANGING

The Second World War brought a halt to new house building and to the slum clearance programme itself. By 1945 overcrowding was once again a problem, and the intervening years had done nothing to improve the condition of older properties in the Wharf Street area. According to one description of typical dwelling in 1947, *"the house comprises four rooms. The street door opens into the downstairs living room... Under the stairs is a larder which has no ventilation. One of the two bedrooms is a small box type room. There is no piped water or water closet in the house...".*

SLUMS ARE BEING TORN FROM THE GROUND

However, urgent as it might be, the slum clearance programme could not resume immediately after the war. Building materials were restricted, labour was in short supply and funds were limited. It was not until the early 1950s that plans were drawn up to redevelop around 27 acres in the Wharf Street area, containing over 1200 properties.

Some of those displaced were rehoused on new Council estates in outer areas of the city, such as New Parks, Thurnby Lodge and Eyres Monsell. However, it was also proposed to build houses and flats on part of the cleared site itself. According to a survey by the Council's Slum Clearance Committee, many of the inhabitants of the Wharf Street area themselves *"expressed a wish to remain in that vicinity... and enquiries made by the Housing Manager demonstrate conclusively that there is a preference for a house with a garden rather than a flat...".* As it was, the higher subsidies offered by central government for flats as against houses proved the deciding factor, and the final development consisted of a mixture of three-bed maisonettes, and one and two bedroom flats. A substantial proportion of land was also reserved for industrial units, intended to house at least some of the 200 firms whose premises were demolished to make way for the clearance scheme and a new ring road.

Once the decisions were made, the work proceeded at a great pace. *"DAY BY DAY THE FACE OF LEICESTER IS CHANGING"*, reported the *Mercury* on 4 December 1957:

St Matthew's Church and new housing on St. Matthew's Estate in 1972 (Leicester Mercury)

"Daily Leicester people can see history being made... Soon work will start on the new St. Matthew's Estate, to eradicate for all time the cancer that was the old Wharf Street area... Over one thousand seven hundred houses have been demolished since 1955. A magnificent total, when it is realised that in Nottingham, a City of comparable size with similar problems, only 131 have been pulled down...".

Mrs Norma Jinks *"watched every bit of it going up brick by brick, I think because we wanted one of those so badly at the time. You had to supply all sorts of details about yourself, where you worked, how much your income was, you had to provide marriage lines. Before they could even think about getting you one, we were well and truly vetted... after you had been in so long they came round again to make sure you weren't doing anything that you shouldn't be doing...".* As the St. Matthew's oral history also recalls, some tenants found the Council rules very restrictive:

> *"Do not walk about the floors without carpet slippers, no carpets or lino to be placed on Marley tiles, no washing or any other objects to be placed on balconies, dustbins to be cleaned out every week... as was the main staircase to be cleaned by everybody as well. Nobody came round to do that sort of thing... You weren't allowed to shake a rug, or a mat or anything upstairs. You had to go down and do it in the blue brick area and woe betide you if you did put one over the railings. I remember one lady who put a small doormat over the railing and just swept inside her porch when the housing lady came along and threw it over the top and said 'That's the place for them, down there!'...".*

In 1958 rents on St. Matthew's were around 30s 6d (£1.52p) for a two-bedroom maisonette, compared with 25s (£1.25) for a two-bedroom pre-war Council house and less than 15s (75p) for an older privately rented house with a garden. *"Materially"*, wrote the Leicester historian Jack Simmons, *"it is obvious that a flat on the St. Matthew's Estate is incomparably better than a house in Wharf Street. It is new; and it is furnished, to an architect's design, with all the private services that can reasonably be looked for...".* Even so, many tenants were sorry to see Wharf Street itself come to such an end. *"Well, it were sad when everybody were moving"*, said one, *"you'd lived there such a long time and you had such fun with one another, and the kiddies had been brought up together and we were moving into different estates...".*

On 3 September 1955, the *Leicester Mercury* published an epitaph of its own. *"I took a stroll around the Wharf Street area yesterday afternoon"*, began its report:

"What a change is taking place there. The once bustling street where years ago small traders made tidy fortunes, is at a standstill compared with what one can recall. In other days, it had such a glorious mixture of shops, butchers, poulterers, not forgetting the rabbits, general grocers, green grocers, and all the rest, with a liberal sprinkling of pubs. And time was when some people in the sedate parts of Leicester sent to Wharf Street for their best steak and roasting joints, because the butchers there would buy a good beast... In those days, the shopkeepers in Wharf Street did more business on Saturday night open until 11 o'clock, and on Sunday morning, than they did throughout the rest of a week...

"I turned into Eaton Street, half-way along Wharf Street. Under yesterday's evening sun, Eaton Street would have tempted an artist. It should be painted now, sleeping whilst it dies. Here was a long street of empty houses, windows broken, whole window frames out in places, and doors off their hinges - a crumbling legacy of the piping days of industrial expansion... Here I found Hope's Place. The name is neatly engraved on a slate tablet over a passage-way leading to a yard and outhouses and what appears to have been a tiny garden, which served the six houses of Hope's Place. The date on the slate tablet is 1821, and this must be an indication of the age of most of the property at the Wharf Street end of Eaton Street...

Part of the St. Matthew's Estate on Wharf Street in May 1995. The flats originally had flat roofs. The building to the right was Marvin's furniture store on the corner of Brook Street. (Leicester City Council)

"In the year Hope's Place was built the town was lit with gas. The population was 30,125. Now Mr George Benjamin Mattock is the last occupant of Hope's Place. He is waiting for a bungalow. Where he is, he looks out upon the blank staring windows of the houses opposite; upon a street where the grass is now growing between the granite square sets; and from his back door he views a scene of desolation...".

Bleak view of St Matthew's Church from Russell Street in February 1957 (Leicester Mercury)

WHAT WAS WHARF STREET?

Wharf Street had a reputation for being a "rough" area, where "outsiders" went at their peril, and even the police went in pairs. The people who lived there were well aware of this.

In the 1930s and 40s, remembers one of them, *"when we were teenagers and that, we used to go dancing, you know. You never told anyone you came from Wharf Street, 'cos it had a bad name. You used to say you didn't live down there... if you picked someone up at the dance, you see. You'd maybe walk a bit further off, you'd never say you lived in Wharf Street, 'cos it had such a bad name".* Even when they moved to another area, this reputation followed them, and *"people held it against you, coming from the Wharf Street area".* But was this "bad name" deserved? *"No! I honestly do not think so",* said Mrs Pettitt:

"And in any case, compared to today...! I mean... I'm not saying it wasn't perhaps rough after the pubs was shut... But otherwise, no, you could go down there and nobody would bother you at all. I never could understand why they said it was a bad area... further down on Russell Square, it might have been a bit rough there, because they had a lodging house or something... I don't know because we didn't go down there at night. But as far as Wharf Street itself was concerned, I can honestly say I never saw any trouble...".

As this suggests, the residents drew their own distinctions between the "rough" and "respectable" parts of the district. The former was very much confined to the Russell Square and Britannia Street area, but families as well as streets were classified in the same way. *"There were some rough lots, same as there is today. Certain families were known to be that way",* as Ernie Martin said, but overall *"it wasn't such a bad place... There used to be the odd fights, you know, but it wasn't as bad as some of the estates are nowadays... My mother used to leave her rent money or insurance money on the table and the rent man or that would just open the door, walk in, take the rent or sign the book, you know...".*

Money aside, *"we had nothing much worth stealing",* as someone else put it, *"but we were all in the same boat, and you'd be lower than low to steal from people who were as poor as you were".* This picture is reinforced by people who lived elsewhere but knew the area well. *"There really was very, very little trouble in that kind of district",* says Margaret Zientek of the time she spent as a teacher at St. Matthew's Infants':

The closure of St. Matthew's Infants' School in 1957. Margaret Zientek is on the right of the cake, and the last Head, Miss Doris Sponton, on the left. (Mrs M. Zientek)

"because they knew you and you knew them... I mean, I taught there 11 years, Lucy taught there 25 and Louie taught there 25 years, and nothing ever... I mean, you'd stay alone in that school, and you didn't necessarily think about locking the front door. You never thought anybody would walk in... you really didn't think anybody would walk in and harass you, or anything like this".

"It was a very poor area, but not much crime. Most folk were typically friendly Leicester people", wrote Rev. Smith of his time at Carley Street chapel. *"It was a very poor area"*, said another member of the congregation, *"but very, very little crime, and the spirit of the community was great"*. No one has claimed that Wharf Street was ever crime free - but what area was? *"I remember a little three year old sitting in front of me.."*, Margaret recalls: *"This little girl sat there one day and she says 'My Dad went out on a job last night'. And Norah (another teacher) said 'I can tell you what sort of job that was!...'. There were some old rogues down there, but I think the crime was fairly minor...".*

So was it true that the police never ventured there alone? *"On Friday and Saturday nights"*, said one former policeman, *"in the Wharf Street area in particular, you coupled up with another PC. You could guarantee at least one good punch-up... helmets and fists flying"*. Wharf Street might have been associated "in particular" with weekend punch-ups, but they were clearly far from unusual in other areas of Leicester - and the police apparently felt safe enough during the rest of the week. *"As for saying the police always went round there in pairs, I don't believe it!"*, said Mrs Pettitt: *"I think, in any case, if there'd been any trouble the old shopkeepers themselves would have soon sorted it out, because they were that type of people... if anyone had started like they do now on any old people, or children, they'd have been in a ruck. They would have capped it!".*

Informal "sortings out" were one way in which people living around Wharf Street regulated each other's behaviour. However, effective policing depended less on force of numbers than the ability to defuse potentially difficult situations, and local knowledge and personal contact played an important part in this. *"The police had a pretty good idea what was going on..."*, said one woman who used to live in the area: *"feuds or whatever... they would talk to the shopkeepers and the publicans, and people out in the street, and very often they could sort things before they got out of hand"*.

Given the cramped conditions in which most people in the Wharf Street area lived, it was difficult to avoid close contact with neighbours, but this was also encouraged by a lack of the money needed to spend their leisure further afield. *"At night..."*, Mrs Pettitt recalled:

> *"I'm talking about when I was a little girl now, at night if it was nights like its been... warm and that, people would sit on their steps, and they'd bring perhaps a jug of beer for the men, bread and cheese, you know, sit and have their supper on the step, and everybody would be talking, kids would be playing, and we'd be allowed to play out, skipping or playing ball... you see, the kids can't do that now, that's the pity"*.

> *"There was a wonderful spirit of a whole district, grannies, aunties and uncles - it was very, very neighbourly"*, remembers Margaret Zientek. People *"went in and out of each others"* houses as if they were their own"*, said another - though not everyone welcomed this constant coming and going. *"One of the best things about moving to Braunstone"*, said one man, *"was having a bit of privacy. You could shut your front door and people didn't keep walking in and out without so much as a 'by your leave'... !"*.

Disputes between family or neighbours were far from unknown, but these were tempered by the knowledge that, in the absence of other sources of aid, people were very dependent on each other for help and support. *"Poverty bred roughness"*, said one man: *"You had to be tough to survive. There were lots of rows, but everyone was in the same boat, not competing with each other. They looked after each other"*.

Different members of the same family often lived close to each other. *"Girls would try to get a house near to their mother when they got married"*, and move back in with her if the marriage broke up for any reason. The feeling that *"your life was never your own"* might be the other side of this particular coin, but mothers and other female relatives were an important source of child care,

Russell Square at its junction with Wharf Street and Bedford Street in May 1995. Dakin's shop used to occupy the building in the centre. (Leicester City Council)

enabling younger women to continue working and contributing to the household finances. Neighbours might also perform the same service, as well as helping out in a crisis - knowing that the favour would be returned when needed. *"Anybody in trouble, I mean, anybody in the street would help you"*, said one woman who now lives on a modern housing estate, *"but now you could be in here for I don't know how long, nobody would know..."*. *"The people..."*, said a former shopkeeper, *"you've no idea how lovely they were... I don't care what people say about Wharf Street... the people were wonderful, they really were"*.

Memory may be selective, but it should be clear from this book that the people of the Wharf Street area have not remembered only the good times and conveniently forgotten the bad. The eternal struggle to survive on a low income, the making do and doing without, the humiliations and the missed opportunities which went with being poor have been described at length - but despite everything, they do have happy memories of their time there, along with a real sense that something of great value was lost when the area was "cleared".

Successive Medical Officers of Health saw Wharf Street as a sanitary problem, and set out to solve it. They studied its environmental defects in some detail, but wasted little time on the people who lived there, except as they featured as impersonal statistics of death and disease. The people who did live there saw themselves as part of a community - a network of mutual dependence and obligation, shared experiences, *"a locality with sentiments, traditions, and a history of its own"*. They were *"all in the same boat"*. None of them want to return to the two-up, two-down and the days before the Welfare State. Even so, the process of saving them from some of the very real threats which poverty posed to health is also seen - rightly or wrongly - as destroying this "community" and everything that went with it. This sense of loss is as much a part of the history of Wharf Street as anything else.

Ernie Tait, who has recently retired after many years' work for Age Concern in Leicester, wrote a brief memoir of Wharf Street which may serve as an appropriate conclusion:

> *"My memories of Wharf Street started in 1947 when I met an elderly lady whose name I have never forgotten - Euphemia. A very nice lady in her seventies... Euphemia's shopping bag had broken, and I carried her groceries home for her. Our meeting resulted in my decorating her one downstairs room. A friend of hers, who lived in Wheat Street, was desperate for someone to carry out a few jobs around the house - so started my career working with retired people.*

> *"Wharf Street with its maze of streets - Wheat Street, Lead Street, Providence Place, Christow Street - all bring back happy memories of warm kind-hearted people. There were no problems getting volunteers to help out a neighbour. The houses may have been old, but the community spirit was magnificent. What a pity it became necessary to pull it down".*

APPENDIX

WHARF STREET.

(84 Humberstone gate.) Wg.
1 Preston W. & Son Ltd. elastic web manufacturers
1½ Kirkland & Tyler, shoe mercers
Potter street—
3 & 5 Holyland Alfred, sewing machine manufacturer
7 Jacobs Samuel H. tailor
Erskine street—
9 Thomson Jn. Edwd. greengro
11 Hardy Geo. H. jun. hairdrssr
13 Cropper Leonard, outfitter
15 & 17 Goodacre John Robert, hardware dealer
19 Dixon Mrs. Tamar Marie, drapr
21 Goodacre & Thompson, drapers
23 Hewitt Alfd. dairyman
25 Williams Mrs. Rose, butcher
Gladstone street—
27 Leicester Hippodrome Co. Ltd. cinematograph hall
27a & b, Lief Harry George, sen. pawnbroker
29 Kays Ltd. grocers
31 Cox James Thomas, baker
33 Cooper Wm. Jas. leather dealr
37 National Provincial Bank Ltd. (sub-branch)
Crafton street—
Wheat street—
47 Turner Percy, beer retlr
49 Adams Mrs. Harriet, florist
51 Berry Mrs. Sarah Ann, draper
57 & 59 Stevens Horace, fruiterer
63 Mansfield John, fishmonger
Carley street—
67 Rodwell Leonard, v. George IV
69 Holt Herbt. newsagt
69 Town Sub-Post, M O. & Telephone Call Office
71 Holyland Albt. Hy. hosier
73 Goadby Jsph. boot mkr. & dlr
75 & 77 Goadby Miss Ida, draper
79 Philpott Chas. Herbt. confctnr
81 Dixon William, butcher
Metcalf street—
83 Cornish Orrill, fish fryer
85½ Barclay Arth. S. furn. brkr
87 Bird Nathnl. clothier
87½ Freer Ernest Walt. & Sons, butchers
89 Badger L. engnr
91 Brown Harry, toy dlr

93 Waring Jn. Thos. v. White Hart
Eaton street—
95 Best of All Boot Repairing Co. Ltd
97 Jackson Wm. & Son, painters
101-103 Franks John & Reginald, house furnishers
105 Hutt Thos. v. Generous Briton
Brook street—
107 Measures Harry, china & glass dealer
109 Clifford Rt. cycle agt
111 Pedley Miss Mary Ann, confr
115 Marston Mrs. Annie, clothier
117 Smith Arth. Edwd. cycle dlr
119 Ward Jsph. Wm. corn dlr
121 Wake Mrs. Marguerite, china & glass dealer
123 Mansfield Herbt. fishmngr
125 Mansfield Stanley Wltr. greengro
Denman street—
127 & 129 Arnold Arth. wardrobe dlr
131 Bird Nathnl. clothier
133 Bendry Mrs. Julia, butcher
135 Overton Samuel, haberdasher
137 & 139 Overton Rt. ironmngr
141 Jinks William Hy. coal dealer
143 Hubble Mrs. Georgina, shopkpr
145 Brown Wm. Hy. watch maker
147 Stanley George, confectioner
149 & 153 Newman Fredk. wardrobe dealer
151 Grimmitt Mrs. Maria, wardrobe dlr
157 Blair Mrs. Emma, umbrella repairer
159 Cole William, watch maker
161 Needham William, shopkeeper
163 Weston & Sons Ltd. grocers
Russell street—
Russell square   (Cross over
202-204 Dakin Robt. Jn. genl.drpr
200 Gregory Horace, greengro
196 Robinson Edwn. Hrbt. grngro
192 Taylor James, news agent
188 & 190 Elliott Leonard, draper
186 Shaw Geo. fruitr
178 Blair Gilbert, furniture dealer
172 Rasdall Herbt. greengro
Upper George street—
170 Beaumont Drug Stores
168 Loseby P. Carr, fever powder manufacturer

166 Garner Mrs. Clara, draper
Wharf street cottages—
162½ Blackwell Horace Edwin, greengro
162 Clark Geo. Fredk. butcher
160 Clifford Jas. Wltr. shopkpr
158 Alliance Meat Co. butchers
156 Measures Arthur, confectioner
154 Hurst Samuel, boot maker
152 to 136 Marvin's Ltd. drapers
Bow street—
134 Hillyer Jsph. Hy. pork butchr
132 Crossley Wm. general dealer
130 Hensman Arthur, retail ironmonger
128 Leicester Co-operative Society Limited Meat Store
126 Leicester Co-operative Society Limited Grocery Stores
124 Blackwell John, fruiterer
122a, Gray Geo. Fredk. v. Jolly Angler P.H
120 Taylor Oliver, boot maker
118½ Boulter Alfred, bookseller
116 & 118 Worthington's Cash Stores (1930) Limited
Pike street—
114½ Sun Kist Fruit Stores, fruitrs
114 Dakin Mrs. Florence, fish frier
112 Idiens George, butcher
110 Veasey Chas. grocer
108 Rudkin Stephen, jeweller
106 White Ted, hairdrssr
102 & 104 Barratt Mrs. A. M. who. newsagt
Old Milton street—
100 Miller Samuel, tailor
98 Idiens William, pork butcher
96 Taylor George, boot repairer
94 Ross Chas. Hy. & Son, butchrs
92 Bloxsom Miss L. milliner
88-90 Moody John G. wholesale & retail tobacconist
86 Moody Harold Alex. hair drssr
78 Reynolds John, v. Green Man
76 Quick & Wearwell, boot reprs
74 Ingram Mrs. Louisa, butcher
72 Plean Harry, baker
68 & 70 Meadow Dairy Co. Ltd. dairymen
Fleet street—
66 Phillips W. & Sons, china & glass dlrs
64 Hill Jn. draper
62 Goffey Frederick, hair dresser

60 Matthews & Leslie, wallpaper mers
58 Melias Ltd. grocers
56 Neale Maurice, confctnr
54 Heggs Mrs. Gertrude Florence, draper
52 Dexter William, fishmonger
50 Lumb Arthur, fruiterer
48 Sarson Mrs. Elsie, news agent
46 Mortimer Ronald, butcher
Lee street—
44 Booth James, cycle repairer
42 Willow Welford Electric Laundries (branch)
40 Smith Luther, fried fish dealer
38 Hutt Mrs. F. confctnr
32 Rushbrook Herbt. coffee tavern
Kenyon street—
30 & 28 Knight Henry Saml. grocr
26 Brooks C. confctnr
24 Shield Arthur, pork butcher & bacon curer
22 Tallis Wm. v. King George III
Eldon street—
20 Hurst Andrew, fish frier
18 Bateman Mrs. Peter, grindery dealer
12 York Walter, hard confectioner
8, 10, 14 & 16 Stevenson Frank, furniture dlr
Camden street—
6 Insch John, herbalist
2c & 4 Adams Walt. boot & shoe dlr
2b, Taylor Arth. newsagt
2a, Ball Nathan & Son, watch mas
2a, Ball William
2 Broome Miss I. A. milliner

From: *Kelly's Directory of Leicestershire and Rutland* (1932)

FURTHER READING

Much of this book is based on tape recorded interviews which form part of the archive of the Living History Unit. These can be consulted by arrangement.

Additional information about the Wharf Street area in particular, and 20th century Leicester in general, can be found in the following:

Primary sources and newspapers

Borough of Leicester, Health Reports; Minutes of the Education, Health, Housing & Slum Clearance & Re-development (Special) Committees; Leicester Advertiser; Leicester Chronicle; Leicester Evening Mail; Leicester Herald; Leicester Mercury. Log Books and other records from local schools can be consulted at the Leicestershire Record Office, which has a number of photographs and other documents relating to the Wharf Street area. Street directories such as Kelly's and Wright's are an invaluable record of change in the Wharf Street area, as well as including much incidental information about local churches and schools. These are also available at the Leicestershire Record Office.

Books and pamphlets

Leacock H. & R., *The Theatre in Leicestershire* (1986)
Nash D. & Reeder D. ed., *Leicester in the Twentieth Century* (1993)
Simmons J., *Leicester Past & Present,* Vol. II (1974)
Snow E.E., *Leicestershire Cricket* 1947-1977 (1977)
St Matthew's Tenants' Association, *St Matthew's Oral History Project* (1991)
Willbond B., *A Home of Our Own* (1991)
Williams D., *Cinema in Leicester* 1896-1931 (1993)